A Time to Grieve

A Time To Grieve

*Meditations for healing
after the death of a loved one*

Carol Staudacher

Hallmark

HarperOne
An Imprint of HarperCollins*Publishers*

Grateful acknowledgment is given for permission to reprint the following:

Quotes from Nancy Hale, Doris Lessing, Vera Randal, and Dr. Joyce Brothers from *The New Quotable Woman,* by Elaine Partnow. Copyright © 1982 by Elaine Partnow. Reprinted with the permission of Facts On File, Inc., New York.

Quotes from Mignon McLaughlin, Linda Hogan, and Anaïs Nin from *Write to the Heart,* by Amber Coverdate Sumrall. Published by The Crossing Press, Freedom, California. Copyright © 1992 by Amber Coverdale Sumrall and reprinted with her permission.

This edition published in 2012 by Hallmark Gift Books, a division of Hallmark Cards, Inc.

Visit us on the Web at Hallmark.com.

ISBN: 978-1-59530-530-5
Printed and bound in China
BOK1202

This book is for all survivors who are grieving the loss of a loved one, and for those whose loved ones died some time ago but who have not given themselves a time to grieve.

Contents

Introduction

The death of a loved one is, for most of us, the most profound emotional experience we will ever have to endure.
Dealing with the deep and prolonged grief that follows such a
loss may well be the most painful and disturbing challenge of
our lives.

This book accompanies you through this difficult period.
The meditations contained in these pages speak to the personal
concerns of all survivors. Written to connect with you wherever you are in your grieving process, these meditations are
appropriate *regardless of when your loved one died.* As long as
you are still feeling the effects of the loss—as long as you are
still coping with feelings of sadness, guilt, yearning, anger,
confusion, fear, or any of the many other grief-related responses—you will find meditations here that will speak directly to your experience.

Each page begins with a quote from a survivor who was,
like yourself, coping with the death of a loved one. You will

find that these survivors' responses and concerns are very similar, if not identical, to your own. For even though each death has its own unique characteristics and each survivor has special circumstances and reactions with which to cope, there is also a wide range of grief responses common to all losses.

You are likely to identify more with some of the survivors' statements than with others. Some of the statements may be ones you could have made yourself. You may, for example, feel a kinship with the teacher and surviving mother who said despairingly, "Since the death, my whole world has fallen apart." You may echo the questions asked by the middle-aged widower whose wife died of cancer: "When will this grief ever end? How long does this go on?"

Unfortunately, grief does not have a set schedule. There are no deadlines for the resolution of loss. Instead, the grieving process consists of three broad and overlapping phases: *Retreating, Working Through,* and *Resolving.*

In *Retreating,* the first phase immediately following a loved one's death, we experience disbelief, shock, confusion, and disorientation, as well as a number of other reactions.

In the second phase, *Working Through*, we experience the full impact of our loved one's death. We find that we need to cope, on a daily basis, with a variety of feelings, reactions, and conditions that we would never have imagined possible. Our lives begin to undergo change as we grapple with all that the loss means to us and all that it causes us to *feel* and *think* and *do*. This is the most crucial phase of the grieving process, during which our feelings and responses need expression and release. It is a time full of repetition. We tell our stories over and over. We ask ourselves the same questions again and again. We confront longing night after night and day after day. And as we repeatedly experience the same emotions and conditions, we need to talk about them, too. We benefit during this time from seeking and accepting the support of others.

In the final phase, *Resolving,* we are able to integrate the loss into our lives. We begin to see that we are going to go on, to move forward in our lives. We have days of hope—even days of excitement and pleasure. This does not mean that we *no longer care about* or *have forgotten* our loved ones. It simply means that we have progressed through recognizing the loss, releasing our grief, expressing our sadness and despair and longing, and all the myriad of feelings that result from being a survivor. When a loved one's memory becomes a part of our ongoing lives, that memory will help to sustain us. As one survivor put it after the death of his wife: "What I feel now, more than anything, is gratitude, tremendous overwhelming gratitude that I had such a person in my life. After the pain of grief, that gratitude inspires me every day and gives me energy as I reenter the world."

The survivors whose voices provide the inspiration for these pages are people who lost spouses, children, parents, siblings, friends, or lovers. Their loved ones died as the result of illness and disease, accidents, suicide, or murder. These survivors represent a wide range of ages and backgrounds, religions, ethnicities, and occupations. But they all had one experience in common: a sense of profound loss after their loved one's death.

May you gain strength from their voices and the meditations that parallel their concerns. And, as you read, may you gather hope, find the courage to express your thoughts and feelings, persevere through the ongoing release of your grief, and eventually find freedom from emotional pain.

How to Use *A Time to Grieve*

This book is divided into three sections that correspond to the three broad and fluid phases of grief: *Retreating, Working Through,* and *Resolving.* The meditations found within each section present a wide variety of survivors' expressions and an extensive range of topics. Although the topics are arranged to correspond to the grief phases in which they are most likely to occur, the meditations are not meant to be read in any specific order. In other words, this is not the kind of book that should be read progressively, from front to back. To find your starting point, you can consult the topic index or simply skim the survivors' quotes at the top of each page until you see one that speaks to you.

One day, you may find yourself drawn to a certain topic in one section that addresses your needs; the next day, you may see that you are connecting more with a topic in another section of the book. You will find it most rewarding to select meditations that best match the way you're feeling on any particular day. This book is designed to be used as it suits you best, the way it speaks most directly to your feelings, moods, wishes, dreams, and concerns.

It is the aim of *A Time to Grieve* to assist you, to be your companion, as you make that difficult but necessary and rewarding journey from coping to healing.

ONE

Retreating

I need to keep my mind clear and just think this through.

All great discoveries are made by [people]
whose feelings run ahead of their thinking.

C. H. PARKHURST

*S*ome survivors try to think their way through grief. That doesn't work. Grief is a releasing process, a discovery process, a healing process. We cannot release or discover or heal by the use of our minds alone. The brain must follow the heart at a respectful distance. It is our hearts that ache when a loved one dies. It is our emotions that are most drastically affected. Certainly the mind suffers, the mind recalls, the mind may plot and plan and wish, but it is the heart that will blaze the trail through the thicket of grief.

❧ *Grief is a discovery process. I will open myself to the discoveries my heart and head will make. Grief is a healing journey, and I will trust my heart to lead my head in this journey.*

I'm afraid to let my feelings go, to grieve. I don't know what will happen to me.

Grief is itself a medicine.
WILLIAM. COWPER

When we suffer any blow, we need to recover, to heal. Grief is the way to healing after a loss. When we are feeling deep, powerful emotions or impulses, it is necessary for us to acknowledge them, knowing they will not harm us. We won't damage ourselves or fall apart if we allow ourselves to feel and act in ways that are dictated by our truest instincts. We cannot constantly hold back, push away, or censor what we really feel. Fearing to grieve gets us nowhere. With grief, the way back is the way through.

∾ *Even though my feelings are turbulent, and at times consuming, I must not fear them. Grieving my loved one will eventually allow me to heal. By speaking when I need to speak and taking action when I need to, I will be contributing to my own recuperation, the eventual resolution of my painful loss. Such a resolution does not mean I will no longer have a bond with my loved one; it means only that I will have begun to see how my life can move forward.*

Since the death, my whole world has fallen apart.

There is something in the pang of change
More than the heart can bear
Unhappiness remembering happiness.

EURIPIDES

When we lose a loved one, almost everything in us and around us seems to change at the moment of the death. We are likely to feel isolated. And we may feel, too, as if the world is a vastly confusing and chaotic place.

We long for just a few moments with our loved one. We reflect on the happiness that person brought into our life. Nothing else makes sense to us but the rare and meaningful relationship, which we cherished—which is now gone. Consumed by our devastating loss and our longing, we see ourselves and the world much differently than we ever have before. From this time on, we think, the world will never be the same. And in a very real sense, our world *is* changed the moment a loved one dies because each person we love makes up a precious and vital piece of our world. At such a challenging time, we need to be patient with the chaos we are now enduring both inside us and around us. We must have faith that it will surely and gradually diminish.

꩜ *The pieces of my broken world will slowly knit themselves back together—not in the same way as before my loved one's death—but in a way that will allow me to live in peace from constant emotional turmoil, to live without daily suffering.*

Things are a mess and it's my fault.

When one does nothing, one believes
oneself responsible for everything.
JEAN-PAUL SARTRE

*I*n the chaos that follows a death, it is easy for us to become inactive and withdrawn. We may be unable to voice our opinions or to express our concerns. We may retreat to the corner of the room and watch the frenzied activities of others. Or we may sit in the center of the group of mourners and do and say nothing. Most likely, our efforts at any conversation or action will be minimal during the first few months after the death. We just get through each day any way we can.

Yet, whether or not we participate in life, it continues to go on around us. And all of the daily fallout from life invades our world, whether we want it to or not. We see ourselves as responsible for doing a great deal, but actually doing nothing. Sometimes it's as if we have created a great void from which all mistakes and errors in judgment have arisen.

But, of course, our inactivity is not the driving force behind the disharmony, confusion, and mistakes that surround us. Even though we may have withdrawn and we may be doing nothing, that doesn't make us responsible for everything—now, or at any other time.

❧ *Because I have temporarily retreated from the life that goes on around me, I feel personally responsible for everything that isn't going well or doesn't turn out the way it should. I feel I could have made it right if only I had participated. I need to give up these feelings. They do not accurately reflect what is really happening. Death creates chaos, regardless of what I do or don't do. It isn't realistic for me to think I am responsible for everything and everyone around me.*

I just can't deal with it right now. It's too much for me to handle.

Denial is only anxiety management.

ANONYMOUS

It is natural to turn away from death after it first occurs, possibly to the extent of denying that our loved one has died. We hear about the death, or see it, and then a part of ourselves shuts down.

But there is a reason for this: it happens because we can't tolerate the thought of our loved one no longer being with us, no longer being available. We can't tolerate what this death will make us feel. We can't consider the impact that the death will have on our lives. We can't fully accept all that information at once.

Such reactions are nature's way of protecting us when we need to be protected. We deny the complete reality of the death and let it in only partially and very gradually, in amounts just large enough for us to deal with successfully. It's as if our hearts and minds have a quota for emotional pain, and that is what we allow ourselves for a day or an hour. When we *can* handle it, we link up with the reality of the death; we consider its many aspects and the ways in which we are directly involved and affected. We feel the necessary pain.

❧ *I am unable to cope with this death right now. I will not force myself. Instead, I will allow myself some time to get accustomed gradually to the shock I have experienced. I will be kind to myself and trust myself to incorporate the fact of this loss at the rate at which I can deal with it.*

Death was something that happened to other people. It was not going to happen to anyone I loved.

I learned early to keep death in my line of sight, keep
it under surveillance, keep it on cleared ground and
away from any brush where it might coil unnoticed.

JOAN DIDION

*U*ntil death enters our lives and takes someone we love,
most of us think of death as something that happens to
someone else. It is not an inevitability, but an aberration. If
thoughts of death enter our minds, we quickly shove them
out. Death, we think, has nothing whatsoever to do with us,
with our lives, or with the lives of the people closest to our
hearts.

Because of this way of thinking, the sorrowful fact of death
occurring in our lives is nearly impossible for us to fathom. We
have great difficulty accepting the reality of the situation. We
feel alienated from what we have always believed to be true.
Because our lives have been altered so quickly and drastically,
we assimilate that change very slowly. This is as it should be.
Little by little, rather than all at once, we come to understand
what has happened to us. To completely grasp what death
means to us in one moment would be impossible. We go gradually through this strange and difficult time. Even if we knew
our loved one was going to die from a terminal illness, the finality of the death is not something we can immediately allow
fully into our consciousness.

ᕽ *My mind will attempt to thrust out the reality of what has
happened to me. I will grapple with the fact of death by trying to
wish it away or drive it out, but it will keep returning. This is all a*

part of the process of loss. It is the part that tries to prevent me from experiencing pain, that holds on to things as they were, rather than looking at things as they are. I will have these tumblings back and forth between what has happened and what I wish to be true. After a time, I will gradually begin the process of acceptance, but I do not have to do it immediately. I can allow myself time.

I wake up in the morning and I still feel as if I'm in a nightmare. I can't believe this has happened to me.

Where belief is painful, we are slow to believe.
OVID

It takes a considerable time for our disbelief to dissolve. Until it does, we seem to be looking at everything through gauze curtains. What we see is not the vision made possible by our real sight. The sounds and words that filter through to us are not the products of our real hearing. The rooms we move our bodies through are alien rooms and the world itself is a strange place with otherworldly qualities.

These things happen because some protective mechanism within ourselves is continually sheltering us. When we are under its influence we usually don't care much that our vision is dimmed or that our other perceptions are distorted. We feel detached as we experience disbelief at every turn. We wake up every morning to find that odd feeling still with us, and only the smallest voice says: "The terrible thing that happened to you is real. It isn't made up. It isn't a figment of other people's imaginations. It isn't a mistake." So the painful process of gaining clarity and a sense of reality may take months.

It is very difficult to get used to the shock we feel when the fact of our loved one's death is made painfully evident. So when we see something or hear something, when we find that his chair or room is empty, or we answer a phone call and it's someone asking for her, we need to take a moment to ease the jolt, to allow ourselves to pause and take a breather as we move through the shock.

❧ *When I feel the stunning blow of disbelief, I will go to a place where I feel comfortable and rest for a moment or take a short walk until the shock dissipates. I will recognize that these little shocks will happen over and over, but that I will eventually have days that are completely free of them. When they happen now, I will allow a "loving hesitation" in my life—a pause that lets me gather my physical and emotional energy—so that I can meet at least some of the day's minimal demands. I won't try to meet the big ones, only those that are small enough to manage.*

What is this all about? Why do I have to live through this?

Between grief and nothing I will take grief.

WILLIAM FAULKNER

S ometimes it helps to remind ourselves that the reason we feel grief at a loved one's death is simply because we had the capacity to love. If we never experienced love, then we would have no involvement that would be strong enough or deep enough to cause unpleasant emotions. For that reason we can accept grief as a testimony to our capacity to bond with and care for another. It means we have the ability to gain closeness with another, to feel affectionate, to dedicate part of our emotions and energies to another. It is those same emotions and energies that now cause us pain, that come rushing into the void left by our loved one's death.

❧ *My grief is a heavy burden, but it is a burden that serves as proof of a loving relationship. I will remember, as I long for my loved one and experience the many other emotions that make up my grief, that it represents something very important in my life. It attests to my ability to care for and love another.*

The world seems so empty now, as if there is no one in it.

Sometimes, when one person is missing,
the whole world seems depopulated.

LAMARTINE

The loved one who died had filled our world. We were content to be with that one person. There were others around and we cared for them, but our loved one was the center of our universe. And when that center was removed, all else faded away. Now the other people we see and hear have little or no effect on us. We long only for the loved one to come back, to be alive in the world with us.

The death of our loved one, we feel, has diminished the world itself. There are people around us, yes, but they seem inconsequential in our lives.

❧ *When feelings of isolation bear down on me, when I feel as if the very center of my universe is missing, I will recognize that there are others around me for whom I may care and who care for me. I will be willing to accept at least some small degree of attention and affection from them.*

I want to talk to him about the death, to see how he's doing, but I'm afraid.

[Kindness is] the golden chain by
which society is bound together.

GOETHE

S ometimes it takes courage for us to approach the subject of the death with another survivor. But the act itself is one of kindness and concern. It shows we care, we want to help, we want to accompany the other person—at least for a short while—in sorrow.

It is by such acts that we, as survivors, are bound together. It is by such acts that we, as a society, are bound together. Reaching out to another person is never wrong. Showing kindness is never wrong. It may not always be conventional, but it is never wrong. We need to remember to be alert to the feelings and silences and withdrawals of others and to take the first step when we feel it needs to be taken.

❧ *I will seek the strength of an emotional connection with another survivor. I will reach out to the other survivor and ask: "How are you doing? Do you want to talk for a while?" By doing so I will both give and receive support in my grief. I will be thankful that such acts of kindness—both given and received—are possible in the midst of our loss.*

I haven't seen that friend since the death.

Never does one feel oneself so utterly helpless as in trying
to speak comfort for great bereavement. I will not try it.

JANE WELSH CARLYLE

*W*e are sometimes surprised by the occasional close
friend who disappears from our lives after the funeral
is over. This is the person we felt we could depend on, one of
the people we liked the best and trusted the most to come
through. When we sense that we have been deserted, we feel
angry and disappointed. It is only natural that we should be
upset. We feel that the person has been selfish or superficial.

But that is not necessarily true. Some people cannot give
comfort because they were not raised in an environment in
which solace was a part of people's behavior. It is alien to them
to try to extend any deep, sustaining kind of consolation. They
care, but they don't know where to begin. They are afraid of
their own feelings as much as they are afraid of ours. And so
they don't try to make a connection.

We can recognize that others have their limitations and
that their experiences have shaped them differently from ourselves. They are not bad people, they are simply people who—
for one reason or another—are unable to join with us in our
sorrow, and that is what we need most now.

*I will forgive my friend for his or her feelings of inadequacy
and confusion, for not knowing what to do for me or say to me. I will
remember that my situation is very frightening to people who are already distanced from their feelings. Grief signifies the utmost in vulnerability, and I can't expect that everyone will have the courage to
come close to that vulnerability.*

*Other people tell me how bad they feel, but they don't
know what grief is.*

I measure every Grief I meet
With narrow, probing Eyes—
I wonder if it weighs like Mine—
Or has an Easier size.

EMILY DICKINSON

It seems to us that no one can know how we feel. No one
could have suffered as we do. No one is carrying the
weight of a loss as we are. The death of that person who was so
special to us produces a grief that no one can imagine. We tell
ourselves, "Others may think they know, but they don't."

While the death of each loved one is, without question,
unique, there also are some universal characteristics that survivors feel after a death. It doesn't matter where people live, or
what they do, or what religion they are, or whether or not they
are educated: when their loved one dies, some of the feelings
and responses they have after the death are ones that we all
share. For example, feelings of shock, anxiety, despair, confusion, disorientation, and longing are part of nearly every survivor's experience.

∾ *I will recognize that others intend only to ease my sense of
loss, to ease my pain. I will know that their grief may be different
from mine in some ways, but it will be similar in others. The loss of
any loved one is a weight we all bear as best we can in our own way
and without comparison.*

*Her death makes me feel small and helpless, as if I have
no power.*

Man acquires the stature of the
enemy with whom he wrestles.

NIKOS KAZANTZAKIS

When we grapple with the death of a loved one, we are grappling with a formidable opponent. But as we work our way through the most difficult of times, as we deal with this enormous challenge by confronting what we feel and need, we make it possible for ourselves to change and grow. The growth we will achieve is not something we can imagine now, at the beginning of our grieving process. But when we look back a few months from now, we will marvel at what we have been able to do.

❧ *As I face off against this powerful opponent, I know that I have the power to win and that winning will make me stronger. To make progress, I will not deny my grief. I will acknowledge it, struggle with it, and work with it. And when this difficult period is over, I will find that I have gained in stature—not just now, but for the rest of my life.*

Why did this have to happen to me?

If all our misfortunes were laid in one common heap
whence everyone must take an equal portion,
most people would be contented to take their own and depart.

SOCRATES

*D*eath causes us to question many things. We may question the reason for our loved one's death, the reason he or she had to suffer, or the reason we must survive this ordeal. But regardless of how intently we search for answers to such questions, we cannot find them. Why, we lament, do we have to endure this terrible time? What have we done to deserve this? Why are others' lives less difficult than our own?

When we actually look at our lives and the traumas and losses that we have experienced, most of us know that we have had a burden, but it has been *our* burden. It is not one we would trade for that of our friend or neighbor. Given the opportunity to exchange misfortunes, most of us would take our own and depart.

Ꙩ *I will carry my own burden as best I can without questioning why I have been "chosen" to have so much heartbreak in my life. All of us have been chosen for misfortune at one time or another. The road I travel is difficult—sometimes nearly unbearable—but it is mine. And I will own it and realize that it will lead me out of the darkness.*

Even though we had six months to anticipate it, it is still devastating.

Experience is in the fingers and head.
The heart is inexperienced.

HENRY DAVID THOREAU

With enough experience, we learn to do things with our hands and our minds. It is not nearly so easy to learn to accomplish something with our hearts. Even if we anticipated a death because our loved one was terminally ill, or even if we have had losses before, it doesn't mean the heart has "learned" anything in the process. Each time our emotions are involved in any experience, that experience is essentially new to us.

So grief comes to most of us as an overpowering and demanding intruder. We are fledglings at dealing with surviving a death. We wish we knew more or were better prepared, but preparation can only be minimal at best.

❧ *I begin the journey as best I can with the resources I have and the determination to make it through. I recognize that I need to be kind to myself at this time, to cherish my own feelings, and to honor my emotional needs.*

When my husband died, and my friends came and stayed and stayed, I went into the living room and asked them all to leave. My mother thought it was a horrible thing for me to do.

The costliness in keeping friends does not lie in
what one does for them, but in what one, out
of consideration for them, refrains from doing.
HENRIK IBSEN

Wonderful, well-meaning friends may sometimes fail to sense our needs and may ignore our cues, thinking they know what is best for us. A friend may impose himself or herself on us when we cannot cope with company. People may stop by or call too often, or press us for details too frequently, or insist that we eat when we cannot eat or sit when we want to pace. Whatever the annoyance, we can speak out for ourselves. We can say what we want and need at the time. Doing this may be extremely difficult because we are too tired, too sad, too despairing, or too sick to put up resistance; but if we can muster the energy to express ourselves clearly, we will ultimately benefit by doing so.

∾ *I am thankful for the wonderful friends I have, but I must remember that they may not always know what my boundaries are or when I've reached the saturation point in conversation or company. When that happens, I will thank them for their attention and concern and love; then I will kindly but clearly state my needs. And I will not apologize for having those needs.*

They say they want to help, but I don't know what to tell them.

He who would do good to another,
must do it in minute particulars.

ANONYMOUS

*O*ffers for help come to us from various sources. Some offers we know to be genuine; others we think are less sincere. So what do we do? Most of us thank the friends, relatives, neighbors, or co-workers for offering assistance. Then we have difficulty asking anyone for anything, even though we could use help.

When there is the potential for others to take care of troublesome tasks, we should ask them to help and we should be specific about what they can do to make our lives less stressful. We may need someone to make phone calls, babysit, help with shopping, provide transportation for out-of-town relatives, or take care of a multitude of other small errands or responsibilities. It is okay to ask for assistance. If we find ourselves hesitating to do so, we need only imagine that the roles are reversed and the other person is the survivor. Which responsibilities would we be willing to assume for him or her? Those are the things we can ask for—and should.

❧ *When I need something done that someone else can do for me to make my life less stressful, I will ask for assistance. I will be specific about what I need and will not feel guilty for asking.*

I just feel lost.

It is a sea, every direction possible. And
we rock, dinghies of splintery resistance.

SANDRA LAMPE

*I*n the first days of grief, we feel numb, unreal. It seems as if we are floating through the day, going from one necessary task to another, seeing one person and then another with no real recall of what has happened. It's as if we are cast out in little boats by ourselves, and as far as our vision can reach, there is only the sea of sorrow. Nevertheless, we continue day after day.

This feeling of being adrift, of being cut loose, set apart from our normal experiences of people and pressures, persists, and we find our lives filled with unusual demands that go beyond what we think we can bear. But our resilience is amazing. And, weak or not, we survive this way. We don't sink. We may feel as though we will, but we don't. And we won't.

❧ *As I make my way through this most difficult time of grief, I will recognize that the sense of unreality—of feeling disconnected from the world, isolated, and adrift—is to be expected. It will not last for long. Gradually, I will feel more connections, more stability. The numbness and the floating feeling will dissipate and a whole range of emotions will take their place. Right now, I am doing what I need to do. My body is taking care of itself in this way. I cannot and need not try to change it.*

Sometimes I don't know how I'll make it through the night to the next morning.

The only courage that matters is the kind
that gets you from one minute to the next.
MIGNON MCLAUGHLIN

*N*ights are particularly difficult for many survivors—especially those of us who live alone. It is then, when things are quiet and the telephone doesn't ring, that the wrenching loneliness sets in, the missing, the longing, the torment of having to get through another night of grief.

We can make it easier on ourselves if we see the night as it really is. It isn't endless. It isn't a dark foreboding thing that will swallow us up. It is only a collection of hours, which are a collection of minutes. And it is through one minute at a time that we must persevere. We can do that.

❧ *It doesn't matter whether I have a huge amount of courage or a little courage; all I need is the courage to get through one minute at a time, and I can certainly do that—regardless of how frightening or cruel a night alone can seem.*

I sleep for an hour, then I wake up. It goes on like that all night.

Sleep builds stepping stones.

EEVA-LIISA MANNER

*C*hanges in sleeping habits and patterns are among the most disturbing effects of grief. They rank right up at the top, along with digestive disturbances and lack of concentration. Some of us get insomnia, which starts immediately following the death and continues off and on for months. A few of us dream of our loved one and feel nourished by such dreams. But others of us long to see our loved one in a dream and, regardless of how fervently we wish it, it doesn't happen.

Because of this type of disruption at night, it is vital for us to allow ourselves to rest whenever it is at all possible. If we can't sleep at night, we need to try to sleep whenever we can. The possibility of disturbing our sleeping pattern by sleeping in the daytime is less important than having to suffer from the detrimental effects of sleep deprivation.

We can help ourselves sleep by getting some exercise during the day, even if it is only a short walk. And we can't expect our bodies to rest if we try to survive on caffeine or other stimulants. Eventually, if we help ourselves along, our sleeping pattern will return to normal. Sleep will, once again, build its stepping stones across the abyss of nighttime loneliness. It will contribute to our emotional healing as it enhances our sense of well-being.

༄ *To promote my own ability to sleep and to gain strength, I will get some exercise, will not consume excessive amounts of caffeine or other stimulants, and will avoid pushing myself when I know that rest is what I really need. Instead, I will acknowledge that my physical self has been traumatized along with my emotional self. My body deserves the chance to heal and gain strength, and I will help it any way I can.*

I just go on. Numb most of the time, but I keep going.

To live one's life in a body that one cannot feel,
is, I believe, the loneliest loneliness.

JAMES J. LYNCH

*I*f we are numb, we are unaware of our bodies, our feelings, the various life forces of which we are made. To shut out pain, to ignore or dull all emotion, is to shut out the possibility of joy and pleasure, also. We cannot endure for long in such deprived circumstances. The body makes it possible for us to thrive. The body is the physical home of our emotions. Fortunately, we human beings are constructed so that we are able verbally and physically to express feelings, opinions, thoughts, and wishes that concern us.

Grief is isolating. But we compound that isolation if we fail to unveil *to ourselves* the various needs, drives, desires, and apprehensions that require recognition rather than neglect. We need to allow our bodies to feel. By taking the first step of opening up to ourselves, of feeling what is going on inside us, of confronting difficult issues, we are beginning the journey toward healing and away from "the loneliest loneliness."

∾ *I have been numbing my feelings, ignoring thoughts I needed to explore, wishing away entire parts of myself that are valuable and unique. I will, instead, work toward being a whole person. I will allow my body to feel and to express itself. By not doing so, I harm myself.*

I want everybody to leave me alone. I don't need anything. I'm getting along okay.

When we admit our vulnerability, we include
others; if we deny it, we shut them out.

MAY SARTON

*E*very once in a while it is tempting to shut ourselves off and say we don't need anything from anyone, that we're doing just fine and want to be left alone. And yet, on the inside we're scared. Or we're confused, or lonely, or any number of things.

Shutting ourselves off from sources of help is unwise. If we say we don't need anyone, then we're closing ourselves off from others in a self-punishing and unnecessary way. Instead, we can admit how we feel, which lets others in to help us. We can reveal the issues with which we are having the most difficulty. We can discuss the fact that we're not always capable, strong, logical, patient, and all those other things we need to be.

We need to remind ourselves that we don't benefit at all from sealing ourselves up in fortresses of self-determination, which require that we don't show our "soft side" to anyone.

❧ *I will realize that by admitting my very real vulnerability, I am including others in my life. I cannot and will not attempt to go through this grieving process completely alone.*

Going out so soon after the funeral took all the strength I had.

He who is outside his door already has
a hard part of his journey behind him.

*O*nce death touches our lives and we feel changed by it, we are less likely to want to be among others. We don't want to gather up the energy it takes to step out the door. We don't want to leave the safety of our surroundings. We don't want to be exposed. We wish we could stay inside instead of having to go back to work, start attending to errands, or looking after the needs of someone else.

Taking the first step is difficult and can seem risky—even foolhardy—but it is necessary to do, and we can trust in our own strength, courage, and ability to get us through the challenge.

❧ *After the funeral, I may feel as if I want to hide forever, but the circumstances of my life—my job, my relationships, and other commitments—make it necessary for me to leave the safety of my home. I will remind myself that after I leave by myself for the first time, succeeding departures will get easier. And I will remember that once I have gone outside and closed the door behind me, I will have made the hardest part of the journey.*

I'm so tired, I don't want to go anywhere or do anything.

The strongest have their moments of fatigue.

FRIEDRICH NIETZSCHE

*G*rief creates exhaustion. We are tired much of the time, if not all of the time. Sometimes the simplest, easiest tasks seem insurmountable, as if they required great amounts of energy.

There is nothing that says we must accomplish as much during our period of sorrow as we did before the death. At the same time, we cannot simply let our bodies go. Forgetting to eat or refusing to take even a short walk will only contribute to a lack of energy. Living on coffee or snacks will not restore us to a reasonably healthy condition. Ignoring lack of sleep will not cure our insomnia.

We need to let our bodies dictate what we can and cannot do. If we do not feel we can meet the physical challenge of making a trip to the store, tending to an appointment or an errand, or attending a meeting, then we need to *accept* that limitation. And, at the same time, we can assure ourselves that the inability is temporary.

When our emotions are demanding so much of us, we must not forget our physical selves. We need to listen to what our bodies need.

☙ *I will pay attention to my body's signals and will not push too hard. But I will also recognize that I need to help my body regain its strength. I have had an emotional surgery that has been hard on my heart and my soul; I must not similarly punish the body in which I live.*

I feel afraid and I don't even know what I'm afraid of.

No passion so effectually robs the mind of
all its powers of acting and reasoning as fear.
EDMUND BURKE

Sometimes invisible fear can nearly paralyze us. We don't act or think as we once did, because at the base of everything we think or do is an underlying fear. This fear comes from the uncertainty that our loss produced. Often, the death of a loved one takes our confidence and turns it into a lack of confidence; it takes our certainty and changes it to uncertainty; it takes strength and wisdom and reduces them to weakness and unclear thought. And in place of these things we feel have been taken away from us, fear settles in.

We need to recognize that this state is temporary; it has occurred because our private world has been shaken. We need to keep in mind that it is our temporarily weakened condition that makes us fearful. Once we regain our strength, our fears will lose their power. We will be able to reason and act and be unfearful in the ways that we were before the death.

☙ *When I feel anxious or afraid, I will recognize this as a natural part of the grieving process. My powers have been diminished by the death, and my confidence in myself and in the world has been shaken. With time, I will regain my ability to consider an action without having to place it against a backdrop of fear. Such a preoccupation with fear only limits my life and has no realistic place in it. I am, as much as anyone, safe from great harm. To venture out into the world is a healthful act, not an incautious one.*

I don't want people's pity.

He that pities another remembers himself.
GEORGE HERBERT

When we grieve, we want understanding, not pity. Well-meaning friends, relatives, co-workers, and neighbors say things that make us realize they are pitying us—but we don't really feel as if they are understanding us and connecting with us. This is both saddening and disappointing.

But sometimes others' pity can contain more understanding than we may imagine. Because it is from their own hurt that their pity arises, we should not be harsh with those who pity us. It may be the only level at which they can enter our grief. We need to recognize and accept that they most likely are carrying a variety of emotional issues themselves, and they may be able to cope with some but not with others.

☙ *I will not be critical or angry when other people express pity. It is probably the only avenue by which they can make a connection with me. My sorrow may make them fearful of going any further than to pity me—for in pitying me they are responding to a hurt or a void in their own life experience.*

I'm tired of people's questions.

Curiosity, one of the most primitive and persistent of motivations, can be a valuable instrument or a nuisance.

ANONYMOUS

A death always arouses curiosity. Questions typically crop up among the first responses we get after making the announcement. Whether they follow the condolences or precede them, they are right up front in our grief experience.

Sometimes the questions persist inappropriately. For example, people who hear of our loss yet are not close to us may ask about the circumstances of our loved one's death. Even the people we love and care about may ask questions we'd rather not answer, because we don't want to have to grapple with the information the answer conveys. We don't want to say how long it was before the person was discovered. Or we don't want to talk about the reactions of others who were in the room or any number of the intimate details of our tragedy. And we don't have to. We can recognize that curiosity is commonplace, even primitive. But refusal to indulge it is our right.

❧ *If I don't want to answer people's questions or satisfy their curiosity, I don't have to. I will look at the questioner and say, "I feel that particular information is private" or "I can't really discuss that with you now."*

I wish people would think before they speak. Some of the things I've heard in the last two weeks have really hurt me.

Of all cruelties, those are the most intolerable
that come under the name of condolence and consolation.
WALTER SAVAGE LANDOR

*U*nfortunately, there are people who come up with thoughtless and hurtful things to say when they are supposedly consoling us. People who lose children are sometimes told they should be glad they have other surviving children or that they can have more children. Young spouses are told they will marry again, that life isn't over. Children who are surviving the death of a parent are told to take care of one another, as if they could meet each other's emotional, physical, and mental needs. These are all remarks made without much thought—and certainly without empathy.

When we are caught in a situation in which we have to tolerate anecdotes, explanations, or advice we don't want to hear, we need to realize that others' thoughtless actions usually have to do with their lack of experience. People who have not lost a loved one often see grief as a very temporary and a fairly rational process that stops soon after the funeral. They don't understand grief's scope or depth. We can protect ourselves by mentally discarding anything they say to us that is not constructive and supportive.

ᴄ᷈ʋ *I will not be hurt by thoughtless remarks others may make. I won't relive a potentially damaging situation over and over. I will* discard anything I hear that causes me to feel blamed, misunderstood, foolish, or overly needy. When I hear such remarks, I will visualize tossing the statement or question into a trash basket. Then I will recall something else that someone has said to make me feel better, a statement that conveyed understanding and support.

I want to be held. I want to be touched.

The greatest sense in our body is our touch. It is
probably the chief sense in the processes of sleeping
and waking; we feel, we love and hate, are touchy
and are touched through . . . our skin.

J. LIONEL TAYLOR

*D*uring grief some of our needs become dulled, some become heightened. One need that is often more intensi-
fied is the need for touch, to be held or hugged, to have
someone pat us as he or she passes by or hold our hand at particularly stressful times. A woman surviving the accidental
death of her husband said, "I know I could heal faster if I
didn't feel so all alone in my skin." Grief isolates us emotionally, but not being touched can make us feel both physically
and emotionally isolated. So our desire for touch is a real, vital
human need.

In fact, studies on touch deprivation have proven dramatically that being touched contributes to leading a healthful life.
It's important for us to allow ourselves to be in situations
where we receive physical affection from those we care about.
If someone wants to hug us or hold us, we shouldn't worry
about such a gesture making us cry or "break down." We need
to follow our natural instinct to give and receive affection.

In support groups, survivors are more likely to touch, hug,
and give affectionate pats, because they know it is a way of

connecting, comforting, and breaking through that terrible sensation of being all alone in your skin.

ॐ *If I respect and care about the person who offers me affection and if I want to hold hands or hug, I will do it. If I cry, it isn't the end of the world. If I cry, in fact, I am allowing my body two ways of re-pairing itself at once—experiencing touch and releasing tears are both ways of healing.*

I don't want someone to talk to. I want someone to be here, to sit with me and not expect me to talk.

Silence may be as variously shaded as speech.
EDITH WHARTON

*A*lthough it is extremely important to communicate through conversation when we are grieving, it is sometimes just as important to remain quiet. We may have a very strong need to sit silently and review the events surrounding the death, to recall things our loved one did or said. Or we may wish to attempt to sort out confusing aspects of our loss, to try to make plans, or just to feel sorry for ourselves. Such needs and desires are perfectly normal and acceptable. All of this silent sorting out makes up a vital period that may last a few weeks or much longer.

For some of us, silence is our major reaction to loss. And the majority of the time silence should be honored and respected by others. Friends may help us by coming and sitting quietly, making a cup of tea, or joining us in a quiet walk, and it isn't wrong for us to ask for that. We don't have to entertain our visitors. It is okay to desire someone's presence but, at the same time, to wish for that person to remain silent with us.

∾ *When I want someone to share a silence with me, to sit quietly in the same room, to go for a walk without having a conversation, or to hold my hand or put his or her arms around me, I will ask for that. I deserve to be nurtured in silence and to receive gestures of reassurance. When my mental and emotional rhythm calls for silence and warmth, I will respect that need and do my best to fulfill it.*

If only I had . . .

It is only too easy to compel a sensitive
human being to feel guilty about anything.

MORTON IRVING SEIDEN

Regardless of how good we were to our loved one, how much care we took and love we exhibited, how much time we spent with him or her, or how much concern we showed, we can still suffer from guilt.

If only I had *not* done this—or *had* done that, we think. We torture ourselves by reliving, over and over, mistakes we think we made.

But most of us do the best we can at the time we are doing it with the resources we have at the moment. The things we feel guilty about after a loved one's death seldom—almost never—have any validity. Feeling guilty is our way of making ourselves believe that we had some control over the death. We do this because it is difficult to have to recognize that we are living in a world where terrible things can happen that are completely beyond our power to govern them.

ᕕ *When guilt haunts me, I will recognize that it is my way of taking some responsibility for a death when I, in fact, was not responsible. I cannot determine and control the length of another person's life regardless of how much I love that person.*

I can't forget the thing I said to hurt him. I did it on purpose, and I never told him I was sorry.

Men are apt to offend ('tis true)
where they find most goodness to forgive.

WILLIAM CONGREVE

There are probably no survivors on this earth who do not experience regret, even pronounced emotional pain, about some specific thing they said or did when their loved one was alive. It may have been some small thoughtless act; it may have been something calculated to hurt the other person. Then, after it was done, there wasn't an apology. The hurtful thing was never discussed; the air was not cleared.

We may not like to admit it to ourselves, but we often lash out more readily at those whom we know will forgive us. Because they care about us and understand us, we assume they will tolerate more from us—and frequently they do. This thinking on our part is certainly not always conscious. In fact, most of the time it probably isn't, but it permits us to take liberties with our actions and our tongues that we would not otherwise take.

☙ *I will forgive myself and know that I was, in all likelihood, forgiven by my loved one for the uncaring or thoughtless things I said or did. He or she knew what my real feelings were, and the acts that I regret did not reflect those feelings. When I am punishing myself for an unresolved disagreement or an unfortunate act, I need to trust in the goodness of my loved one and his or her capacity to forgive me not once, but as many times as necessary.*

*I try to make myself think about something else,
to be rational, but it doesn't work.*

The head does not know how to
play the part of the heart for long.
LA ROCHEFOUCAULD

*E*ven though we may try again and again to shut down our emotions, to still the miseries of our own hearts, it often does not work. We can make our heads do a great many things, but we can't make them successfully override the grief caused by a loved one's death. Such willful attempts do not work—and there is a very good reason why they don't. If our intellect could reign over our emotions, if we could successfully tell ourselves to think of other things when our grief arose, we would be forever in a state of bereavement. Our grief would go underground and cause difficulties in a great many ways, affecting our emotional swings, our psychological makeup, and our physical health.

∾ *I welcome the messages of my heart. I know they are true and come from the deepest life source I have. While it may seem, at times, that I could spare myself pain if only I could remain in my head, I need to recognize that it is not my intellect that will help me release my grief; it is my heart.*

I think I see him driving down the street or coming in the back door, then I realize . . .

Desire is indeed powerful; it engenders belief.
MARCEL PROUST

We wish so hard when our loved ones are gone, wish we could see them, or find them sitting in a favorite chair, walking through the door, or calling on the telephone at their regular times. It isn't unusual to be thoroughly convinced that we see our loved one driving down the street, waiting for a bus, working in a store, or even entering the front door. In fact, our desire to see our loved one is so powerful it makes us believe, momentarily at least, that he or she is still here, still with us, still capable of a physical presence.

Though these occurrences quicken the pace of our hearts and rouse our hopes, they just as rapidly disappoint us. So eventually we learn to understand them for what they are: the products of our wishful thinking, our desire.

These fleeting glimpses and images may occur quite frequently for a few months, even a year or so after the death. Then they gradually subside. Talking or writing about what we imagine we see can help us to release the disappointment and pain these images cause.

❧ *When I am struck by the appearance of someone who bears an extreme likeness to my loved one, when I am convinced that my loved one is not really dead, that there is a mistake, I will take a moment to lessen the power of that image. I will do this by writing about what I saw, how I felt when I saw it, and how I felt afterward. Or I will relate the story of what happened to a trusted listener. Doing so will help me to focus and release the emotional blow I have suffered.*

I'm so angry at her for leaving me like this. How could she do this to me?

No man is angry that feels not himself hurt.

FRANCIS BACON

We often feel angry for having been deserted. We are hurt to be left alone. We may even wish for the opportunity to express our anger toward the person who died. A surviving spouse may feel abandoned, uncared for, as if the deceased husband or wife would have been determined and able to live longer if he or she had *really* loved the survivor. Such thinking is, of course, unrealistic, but it denies the survivor's grief for a while and puts it aside. That is, anger displaces other feelings that may be much more discomforting to confront. Using anger in this way is the equivalent of changing the subject when we are talking in order to evade the topic under discussion.

When anger occupies our thoughts day after day, it consumes energy, directs attention, and takes up time. We can let our anger out as we need to and talk to other people about our angry feelings, but eventually we need to acknowledge that much of our anger is really just a convenient repository for lots of other feelings.

ᐁ *When I'm angry at my loved one for dying and leaving me alone, I will vent my anger if I am by myself or I will talk to someone about my anger. But because anger is one of the most powerful emotions, it should be kept in perspective. I will ask these questions of myself and do my best to answer them: What purpose is my anger serving? How long do I want to invest my energy in it? What is it covering up?*

I wish I could have died before my loved one.
I never thought I would have to outlive him.

The most I ever did for you, was to outlive you
But that is much.

EDNA ST. VINCENT MILLAY

 We are not prepared, most of us, to be left behind. We thought we would die before our spouse, our friend, our sibling, or our child. And yet, here we are having to cope with this aloneness and loneliness at the same time.

Even though outliving the person we loved was never part of our plan, never part of our expectation, it is, in a way, our gift to that person. It is we, instead of our loved ones, who are experiencing the sorrow.

 I am alone and I am lonely, but if I were asked to decide between being the cause for sorrow or accepting the sorrow of loss, which would I select? I am here to go on, to carry the legacy of my relationship into the days ahead, to make bright my loved one's memory, to see it as a fire from which I can forge a future.

I know I glorify him—but that's my business.

But it's the truth even if it didn't happen.

KEN KESEY

*I*n the first early period of our grief, as we remember our loved one and recall times we had together, we may have a tendency to distort reality, obscure the actual event, or fabricate a facet of our relationship. If we do, there's no harm done. It is our reality for now, and it is one we may need to believe in for the time being. It may not be so far from the truth as to be significant, or it may be drastically different from the facts. Either way, it doesn't matter.

Many loved ones are mythologized to a certain extent after their deaths. Many relationships undergo a transformation of the wishing process. It is all part of our survival. It becomes dangerous only if we create a fiction that we are unable to give up, because that fiction could then make us unable to grieve the real person who died.

∾ *I know I don't always remember things accurately or look at the complete picture when I am recollecting my relationship with my loved one. That doesn't matter. For a while now, I can smile and tell myself "it's the truth even if it didn't happen."*

When she died, my faith was wiped out.

A faith that sets bounds to itself, that will
believe so much and no more, that will trust
thus far and no further, is none.

JULIUS CHARLES HARE *and*
AUGUSTUS WILLIAM HARE

We feel there is no reason for our loved one's death and that if there is no reason, then the death may be considered a punishment. This is particularly true if our loved one died in a sudden or violent way, or died at a young age. Our faith is seriously shaken; in fact, we may feel as if it no longer exists.

But at such times we need to consider that faith applies, always, to something that exceeds the scope of our imagining, to that which is beyond our seeing and our understanding.

We can't place limitations on faith. We can't bargain with any being—earthly or otherwise—and promise to restore our belief if only such and such will happen. True faith does not work that way. If we wish we could have faith but fear that we have lost it, we can remind ourselves that trust is part of hope and hope is part of renewal after loss. Giving up on these steps means giving up on a force larger than ourselves that can offer us much comfort during a lifetime.

∽ *I will not place limits or bounds on my faith. I will not require assurances. I will invest my trust, recognizing that faith itself is a belief that goes beyond my own knowledge and capabilities. If it were anything else, I would not have needed it to begin with.*

I'm trying to decide what to do next, and I don't know. I wish I did.

Living is a constant process of
deciding what we are going to do.

JOSÉ ORTEGA Y GASSET

For some people, losing a loved one seems to necessitate a drastic change, such as selling one's house, moving, or changing a job or lifestyle. Any kind of major change may be tempting.

Similarly, many of us survivors present ourselves with a selection of alternatives. Then we are miserable because we can't pick one. But selecting one excludes the possibility of another—and so it goes, back and forth. It occupies our time and energy. It torments us. We lament: If only we had some way to know which choice would be best for us.

But usually the choice is all too simple—for the best choice is to do nothing. The preferable path is not to get involved in any significant life change for at least one year. If there is no absolute need for change, such as a financial crisis, there should be no moving or quitting or selling. There will be plenty of time for that when we are not experiencing the jumble of feelings created by our loss.

❧ *I am not in a state that allows me to make wise decisions. If I find that I am tempted to alter some area of my life, I will talk my idea over with a helping professional. I will not act on any major change without consulting a party whom I trust and who has not been personally affected by the death.*

I wish I were in a wheelchair unable to move, so people would know what I've been through.

We can see the smoke of a burning home,
but who can know of a burning heart?

MALAY SAYING

The passions of the heart are not always visible, particularly when we are suffering a severe loss. Survivors often say they wish they could wear a sign or a badge to signal to other people how damaged they feel. Grief is isolating and it is deceptive. Sometimes a person who seems perfectly fine on the outside is going through extraordinary inner torment day after day, hour after slow hour.

We can't change the way our culture is. We can't insist on a special signal to the "outside world" that we're in great distress, but we can talk about what burns inside us. We can seek a support group where we will be among others who know how it feels to hold it in, push it down, and pretend everything is okay. By being with others who have gone through a similar experience, we are made to feel less isolated. We can benefit from valuable reassurance and companionship.

༄ *I will not keep silent when I have the need for my loss and my pain to be known. Suppressed grief can lead to illness, and I will contribute to my own health by opening up when I need to.*

I am afraid I'll go over the edge.

Life only demands from you the strength you possess.

DAG HAMMARSKJÖLD

Few of us survivors think we can endure all that will be required from us, day after day. "I won't make it through," we say. Or: "Just one more hour of this, and that will be it. I won't have the strength to go on." But we do. It's as if there is some human formula we know nothing about, and this formula guarantees that the grief, the despair, the terrible mix of emotions that are prescribed for us do not exceed the amount we can handle.

∾ *I will use the strength I have to cope with my circumstances. Somehow, miraculously, the strength I possess will be enough to get me through. If I ever begin to question my own capacities, I will have faith that the resources which are mine, some of which were undetectable before the death, will be adequate and will see me through.*

What can I hang on to?

Hope is grief's best music.

PROVERB

When we are feeling as if there is no way out, nothing to look forward to, and we're anticipating only days and days of emotional agony ahead of us, we need to recognize that we are not alone. There are many others who have been through grief and are now living their lives and functioning as capable, loving people in the world. We will join them one day. After we have been through the challenging tangle of emotions, we will emerge in a clearing where we know the worst is over, and we will feel ourselves gaining the strength to assimilate the changes in our life. We need to carry hope with us, as we traverse the thicket of emotions, and realize that we will, in the future, live a life that is not governed by wrenching emotion.

❧ *As I begin to grieve, I will not abandon hope. I will realize that the others who have made this journey before me have emerged intact. They will give me faith in myself to come through the darkest parts of my life. All the ways in which I have met difficulties in the past and dealt with them will give me renewed belief in my ability to meet the challenge.*

I don't know where I will end up.

Perhaps it happens with us as with the water diviners,
who do not know what guides them to the water, but
something does . . . and twists the wand in their hands.

PRIMO LEVI

*H*ow do we find our way? Where will this sorrow take us? What will happen? Where will we end up? If we trust ourselves, we will tap that which is within us that needs to rise to the surface. We can lead ourselves to it as surely as a water diviner can find water in a forbidding landscape.

There is something instinctive within us that helps us through the most difficult of times and allows us to access our inner strength. We can recognize that our sorrow and our strength come from the same well.

∾ *I will have faith that I can locate the source of my strength and sorrow and that the two will commingle as I heal. For I am able to find my own way, to make my own discoveries, and to benefit from that which I discover.*

People have suggested I go to a support group, but I don't think I would want to be around a bunch of strangers the way I'm feeling.

To know the road ahead, ask those who are coming back.
CHINESE PROVERB

*G*rief crosses all boundaries. Among people who are suffering the loss of a loved one, barriers come down. People we didn't know before are no longer strangers. To be among others who are sharing a similar loss—to learn from others about the process of grief and to hear from them the ways in which their lives could be made less troublesome or painful—is a great gift. Other survivors who have gone before us have tremendous knowledge, support, and comfort to share, and we will benefit by being open and receptive to them.

If we are particularly reticent about committing ourselves to a support group, we can make a deal with ourselves: we will try it and if we don't like it, we won't go again. Chances are, if we attend a few times, we will begin making connections, establishing friendships. We will feel great relief among those who know the road we are on, the rugged terrain over which we will travel, and the time that is required to make the journey.

❧ *I will call a local hospice or the pastoral care office at a hospital to locate a local support group for survivors. I will find out when they meet next and will join in their company at least once or twice. It will be my way of giving myself a new avenue for working through the grieving process.*

TWO

Working Through

The support group has saved my life.

If someone listens, or stretches out a hand, or whispers a kind word
of encouragement, or attempts to understand a lonely person,
extraordinary things begin to happen.

LORETTA GIRZARTIS

A couple who lost their son were drifting apart, unable to
communicate and tired of trying. They had given up on
being able to help one another. Then a friend invited them
to attend a survivors' support group in the community. They
reluctantly accompanied her to the group, but they both remained silent. Throughout the evening, they just sat and listened. When they left, they both felt that the experience had
been extremely exhausting; but, at the same time, they agreed
they had felt a considerable amount of comfort by being
among people who understood what they were going through.
The couple continued to attend the group, and, eventually,
they both began to share their feelings and concerns. They
made friends with the other grieving parents and were able to
gain a new and valuable perspective on how their two differing
methods of grieving were making their marriage unworkable.
The support group saved them from divorce.

We all benefit from being among those who understand,
those who are willing to listen, to stretch out a hand, to whis-
per a word of encouragement. When we are in such an environment, among those who have the experience and capacity

to care in a special way, something extraordinary really does begin to happen.

◯ If I decide to attend a support group, I will do so with no pre-conceived ideas about what I must do when I get there. I will simply go and give myself the opportunity to have a valuable, nurturing experience during a time in my life when I need encouragement and understanding.

*Other survivors have told me I need to tell my story
over and over.*

The universe is made of stories, not of atoms.
MURIEL RUKEYSER

*T*hink about the kind of world we would have if all the
stories of its inhabitants were removed. If we had no individual stories, we would have no culture. We would have no
history. We all know that.

But when we are grieving, it is our *personal* stories, our immediate personal histories that become so important. If we tell
the story of our loved one's death twice a day, three times a day,
or more, and we still have the urge to tell it, then that is what
we must do.

The stories of our love, our life, and our loved one's life are
the most important pieces of information we have. We need to
indulge ourselves, to hear the telling, to listen to our own
words, to say the same thing again and again and again until
we don't need to say it anymore.

∾ *I am the only one who can tell my story—the story of my relationship with my loved one, the story of my loved one's death, and
all that goes with it. In my mind I hold the conversations, the sights
and sounds, the details surrounding the death. It is all right to tell
the story that wells up inside me. I don't need to hold it in and press
it down. I can tell it and tell it until I no longer need to. Each time I
tell my story, I remove one small bit of hurt from inside me. I ease
my wound.*

I feel tormented, even cursed.

Take my word for it, the saddest thing
under the sky is a soul incapable of sadness.

COUNTESS DE GASPARIN

*I*t is painful to feel deeply. Sometimes people who are falling in love say it almost hurts. In fact, a wide variety of feelings can disturb us by their intensity and power. Our emotions sometimes seem to be a curse.

But consider the person who appears to have no great sadness. Look at his or her life. It is not only devoid of unhappiness or despair or longing, it is devoid of pleasure and joy as well. Such a person's capacity for feeling is dulled in every respect. To lead such a life is not an alternative we would freely choose. Given the choice, we would not be souls "incapable of sadness."

∞ *The best I can do when I am being tormented by unpleasant feelings is to put them in perspective: to recognize that they are only part of a whole range of emotions that I am privileged to have. I will accept that I must deal with the most difficult of feelings so that I may enjoy the other, more pleasant ones.*

A man in our support group is keeping a grief journal. He says it helps.

There is a saying that "paper is more patient than man." . . . Yes, there is no doubt that paper is patient and . . . I don't intend to show this cardboard-covered notebook to anyone.

ANNE FRANK

*A*s we experience the feelings and reactions caused by the death of a loved one, we are filled with memories, wishes, dreams, fantasies, insights, questions—and sometimes even answers. We are brimming over with what we have been holding silently inside ourselves. At such times, a journal is an extraordinary friend, a repository for stored thoughts and feelings as well as ones that continue to arise on a daily basis.

Those of us who have kept a journal have found that writing can play an extremely important role in healing—if we give it a try.

❧ *I will locate a notebook that is the right size and color for me, that has the right feel to it, and that looks as if it could be my "confidante." I'll open my heart and mind to paper in a way that I haven't expressed aloud. I'll allow myself complete freedom as I write, knowing that my journal is entirely private. It's a tool to help in my recovery.*

I don't think what I write would make any sense to anyone.

We do not write in order to be understood;
we write in order to understand.

C. DAY-LEWIS

What do survivors write about? Keeping a journal, a log, a notebook, a diary—whatever you want to call it—is a way we can make sense of things, get rid of feelings we don't want to carry, or explore various facts of our lives. We can pose questions. We can revisit the life we led with our loved one. We can attempt to figure out aspects of our relationship. We can express appreciation. The way ahead can be contemplated and examined. Choices can be investigated—all with paper and a pen. No one else needs to know. Writing doesn't cost anything, and it makes possible enormous benefits.

Many survivors, especially male survivors, have worked their way successfully through their grief by writing about it—not in any formal way, but in a daily log or journal. Men who have been very isolated in their grief have found that the sole act of writing daily allowed them to unburden themselves of particularly disturbing and painful feelings and to examine some difficult personal issues.

ᴄᴡ *I'm going to try exploring in writing some of the things that are bothering me most, some of the thoughts that keep recurring even though I try not to think about them. I'll say what I want to say but have been afraid to say. I won't worry about the whole world falling apart around me if I am truthful. I won't worry if it "makes sense," because I'm not going to write for anyone other than myself.*

When I write about what happened to me, I find myself describing feelings that surprise me.

I have found over the years that my
writing has more courage than I do.
LINDA HOGAN

A man who hadn't grieved the death of his son or other family members found that once he started writing about his experience, he described feelings and related events in ways that he had never before considered: "It would have taken so much courage to face those things and to talk about them in the same way when they actually happened. I'm glad I'm able to do it now."

Writing, more than any other activity except conversation, can lead us through unfamiliar emotional territories—through darkness and fear, through anger and frustration, through guilt and confusion, and any number of other grief-related feelings.

We can use it as an effective tool throughout our entire grieving process.

∾ *When I find that I am afraid of something and feel as if I cannot face it, I will find a quiet space for myself and write about my fear or apprehension. I will tell why I feel it and why I think it has power over me. I will reduce it to something harmless through my own written words.*

I don't know how to explain how I feel—worried, afraid, anxious.

Anxiety is fear of one's self.
WILHELM STEKEL

Sometimes our feelings are so hard to pin down, we don't know exactly what they are or what is causing them. We may feel fear but not know its source. We may feel anxiety but not be able to determine the reason for it. All we know for sure is that we feel unsettled.

The most unclear of grief reactions is a low-level anxiety that seems to reside beneath our skin. It is disturbing and perplexing and keeps us from being able to do things we need to do. For example, it keeps us awake, or removes our appetite altogether, or makes us impossibly irritable with others.

This type of anxiety can be the product of a number of fears:

- The fear of falling apart.
- The fear of not making the right decision.
- The fear of not being able to complete something that needs to be completed.
- The fear of what we might say or do in a certain situation.
- The fear of the possible anguish we may be causing someone else.

The list can go on and on. When we feel uncertainty and inner discord, we can ask ourselves if we are afraid of something we believe to be within our power to change. If so, what is it? We need to discuss such fears with a trusted confidante, a support group, or a helping professional. Such unidentified fears can be debilitating and demoralizing, and we don't need to suffer from their effects.

∾ *If I am unable to identify what is causing me to feel continually disturbed, I'll talk it out with someone who can help me gain some perspective on my feelings. There is no need for me to live with feelings of anxiety. By getting help, I can feel clearer and freer and more directed.*

Now I live never knowing who is going to die and when.

Would that life were like the shadow cast by a wall
or a tree, but it is like the shadow of a bird in flight.

THE TALMUD

We have learned that death is unpredictable, illogical, unfair, and sneaky. It pays no attention to age or goodness or faith. We wish for life to be more solid, more dependable, less mysterious in its endings. If only life were like a shadow cast by a wall or a tree, if life were the representation of something solid and immovable, we could be at ease. We could rest assured that all is safe and we are not subject to misfortune.

But if our lives were not like the shadow of a bird in flight, they would not possess the potential for creation, discovery, exploration, and love. For those are the qualities that make life fluid and endow it with all possibilities.

᭡ *I will appreciate my life and the lives of others in a new way and will not invest my time and energy wishing for our lives to be solid, immovable, and unending. For our lives to be so would require removing all the qualities that make life valuable, enriching, and capable of being filled with deep love.*

I just wish there was someone I could punish for this!

I know of no more disagreeable situation
than to be left feeling generally angry
without anybody in particular to be angry at.

FRANK MOORE COLBY

*O*ne survivor described his emotion as a kind of low hum that accompanied him throughout his day. "I would walk around all day," he said, "almost humming like an appliance." That hum was anger. He wanted some specific target, someone to confront, to blame. But there was no one, so in one way or another, he directed his anger at everyone and everything he met.

Living day after day like this creates an unnecessary burden for any survivor. There are many situations and conditions that demand our attention, that require a response and a fairly rational thought process. It is important to remember that anger serves to blur other actions and responsibilities that need to be looked at clearly.

❧ *I will pay attention to the way in which I am approaching others and dealing with them. When I experience difficulty in interactions with others, I will be alert to the fact that it may be because of my anger. I will think about just what the target of my anger is. Then I will focus and safely release my anger so that I may be free to work toward the resolution of my loss.*

I'm feeling hurt and angry, but I'm keeping it to myself.

If you are never angry, then you are unborn.

AFRICAN PROVERB

Some survivors have no trouble talking about anger, exhibiting anger, "working it off," or "running it off." But there are others whose anger causes them to feel shame. They go to great lengths to avoid indicating that they are angry in any way.

As the African proverb points out, if we are alive, we have experienced anger. It is one of the most common human emotions. Unlike fear, love, or joy, anger is, in fact, one of the emotions most frequently expressed by both men and women. You might say that feeling angry once in a while comes from feeling human all your life.

❧ *Most survivors feel anger at someone or something. I won't be ashamed of my anger. My loved one's death has aroused anger in me that I won't deny. I can, if I feel like it, go off by myself where I will not bother anyone and yell and scream until my anger is weakened. I will discuss my feelings with someone whose opinion and experience I value. I will talk about venting anger with the members of my support group. I may even seek the help of a professional. But I will not try to pretend that I have no anger.*

They're responsible for my loved one's death.

To be angry is to revenge the
fault of others upon ourselves.
ALEXANDER POPE

We may feel that it was someone else's negligence or uncaring attitude or ignorance that caused our loved one's death. We are furious because the person's actions were not revealed, stopped, or punished. We feel that the individual—or group or institution—is directly responsible for the terrible loss we are now having to bear.

Sometimes there is a justifiable reason for our anger. But more often our anger is taking the place of other feelings that would be more difficult for us to experience—such as fear or despair. Whatever the reason for our anger and however justified it may be, we need to recognize that the anger is doing us harm. Continually being plagued by anger causes us to overlook positive responses that may contribute more to memorializing our loved one's life. And, equally important, anger can be very debilitating to our bodies. It can cause our physical condition—which may already be weakened by our grief—to be eroded further. We may need to go behind our anger to get at the other critical components of our grief.

∾ *When I am seized by anger, I will stop, take a few breaths, and ask myself, "If I weren't angry now, what other feelings would I be having?" I will recognize that my anger is a mask for those other feelings and that it is those feelings that deserve my attention and expression.*

We had only a few days. I wish I could have spent more time with him before he died.

We do not remember days, we remember moments.

CESARE PAVESE

*M*emories are of tremendous importance to all survivors. They keep us going, give us strength, and can be passed on to others who cared about our loved one. But sometimes we lose perspective about what memories are made of. Those most prominent times that we recall with pleasure, tenderness, devotion, or any number of emotions are ones in which some particular word, gesture, or action embedded itself in our memory. As a result, we have carried those times with us ever since.

The most precious of our recollections do not usually cover long periods; they reflect, instead, brief moments we have selected for one reason or another from the broader segments of time we spent with our loved one. We need not feel deep regret for not having had days or weeks or months to fill our memory bank, when a few moments can stay with us forever.

∼ *I will be nourished continually by the recollections I have of my loved one—moments selected because of their rich personal value. I will realize that, regardless of the length of time I was with my loved one, I now have my own private and unique memories that will continue to reaffirm that I loved and was loved.*

I didn't do enough. I wish I had done so many things while she was still alive.

When we do the best we can we never know what
miracle is wrought in our life, or in the life of another.
HELEN KELLER

ew of us think we did the best we could when our loved one was alive. We may be critical of our own temperament or character. But we need to acknowledge that we—all of us—have our limitations. We often have to operate within a framework that is not of our choosing. Most of us are usually trying to meet the needs of a wide range of people—family, friends, co-workers, and other community members. We can only function as well as possible in the circumstances we're in and with the personal resources we have at the time.

Even so, we may be surprised to find how many of our small acts or gestures and how many of our conversations have positively influenced the life of another person. Something we said or did may have changed the person's outlook on a particular day. Or our action may have been even more far-reaching, influencing the other person for a lifetime.

❧ *When I get discouraged about how ineffective, inefficient, or inattentive I have been and how greatly I feel I failed my loved one, I need to recognize that I may not remember many of the most valuable and supportive things I have done, but they have not gone unremembered by those whose lives have been made richer from my acts. I have acted in the best way I could at a given time, and many times it was more than anyone could reasonably expect. In fact, some of my efforts may have produced wonderful long-term effects of which I am unaware.*

How I wish I hadn't always been so dissatisfied!

Complaint is the sincerest part of our devotion.

JONATHAN SWIFT

*I*t's easy to regret remarks we made as we "picked on" our loved one's faults and criticized behaviors that now seem so unimportant. But the closer we are to someone else, the more we see the things they do, hear the statements they make, observe their habits, and learn about their perspectives and reactions. We know enough about the person to make us love. We know enough to make us judgmental. We know enough, sometimes, to make us critical.

By loving someone we learn their vulnerabilities, and we may take advantage of those when we need to make a point or accomplish a purpose. Sometimes, though, we may complain because doing so is more a habit than a conviction. Regardless, closeness and devotion breed remarks that are both positive and negative. And both are proof of our devotion.

༄ *As I recall the way I interacted with my loved one, I need to recognize that in any close relationship there exists the likelihood of saying too much sometimes. There is even the strong possibility of saying too much too often. That is all part of familiarity. When I start despising myself because I was critical, I'll remind myself of the pleasant, helpful ways in which I interacted, the loving ways I behaved, the things I said and did to enhance the positive aspects of our relationship.*

Why do I feel such ambivalence? I love him and miss him, yet I am angry at him at the same time.

I hate and love. You ask, perhaps, how that can be?
I know not, but I feel the agony.

CATULLUS

We miss our loved ones terribly, and yet we can't shake some feelings of blame, disappointment, or dismay about something they did or that we assume they did. We feel as if there is some unfinished business, something we need to have them say or do to straighten out our feelings about them, to make the memory of them fully loving and positive.

But ambivalence is part of any human relationship. To have an intimate relationship with anyone means knowing that person's faults and weaknesses as well as his or her strengths and virtues. In death, as in life, we recognize both and accept both.

❧ *We acknowledge that we loved a whole person, not a saint, but a real, fallible human being who was subject to all the personal and worldly pressures that influence and weaken us all.*

We didn't always get along. We argued a lot.

Love is the coldest of critics.
GEORGE CURTIS

*L*oving makes us powerful, relentless critics. As a result, we may be left now with the stark memory of a scene we wish we could erase. Or we may be doing silent battle with a conversation raging in our ears that we would rather not hear.

But the love that allowed the closeness that fostered the disagreements is the same love that now takes its toll in other ways. The same closeness that caused unpleasant encounters between the two of us also gave us the joyful experiences and the love that now causes such grief. All of the exchanges we have with our loved ones make up our total experience, and it is that whole experience, with all of its facets, that makes the bond special.

❧ *I will write down each incident that is troubling me now. Then next to it I will write one that I enjoy remembering. When my list is completed, I will have visual proof that in my relationship with my loved one there was a mixture of feelings as well as a range of emotions, opinions, and choices. There will be evidence before me that nothing was all one way or another.*

It's like all the bad stuff never even happened.

That which was bitter to endure
may be sweet to remember.
PROVERB

O ddly enough, sometimes a relationship that was very rocky—even hateful at times—can seem quite pleasant when we look back on it. As we survive the loss of our once-troublesome relationship, it takes on a new character. We actually blank out the worst times and remember the relationship in a different light, recalling only the moments of pleasure.

Such relationships are sometimes difficult to mourn. There may be hidden feelings of ambivalence, or bouts of extreme guilt or remorse. It helps to be aware of the total relationship we had with our loved ones. We need to take into account the good and the bad without feeling disloyal. No relationship is continually perfect, because no two people are continually perfect. By recognizing that our loved one was a whole person with flaws and that we ourselves have deficiencies, we work our way through the grief of a *real* relationship rather than an *imagined* one.

∞ *I will recognize that my loved one was a real person, not a deity, that he or she did not always make me happy or proud. With those limitations, we had a relationship and we were an important vital part of one another's lives. When I mourn, I mourn for the whole person, the real person. I miss my loved one because of his or her uniqueness and place in my life.*

I am obsessed by certain unhappy memories. How can I ever shut them off?

Memory is a treasure of the mind.
ENGLISH PROVERB

Sometimes unpleasant memories that involve our loved one keep coming to the surface again and again. Even though we try to push them away, they return immediately. Because these memories are punishing, sometimes even repugnant, we want to get rid of them, but we are not able to.

But these torturous memories come from the same place where good memories reside like stored treasure. When we feel as if we're being overwhelmed with difficult memories, with things we would rather not focus on, we can imagine opening up another section of our memory, a compartment where all the loving and rich memories are kept. We can imagine uncovering those memories, bringing them to the surface, and validating them. We can let those good memories live.

❧ *My memory is a rich, wonderful resource that brings me much pleasure if I recognize that it retains both pleasurable and unhappy experiences. I will choose to reexamine and be uplifted by the good memories the two of us shared, all the memories on which our love was built.*

I don't think I'll ever be able to forgive her for . . .

Love is an act of endless forgiveness,
a tender look which becomes a habit.

PETER USTINOV

To love is to forgive, because to love fully is to accept the other person unconditionally. Love encompasses compassion, empathy, and understanding. It endows us with the ability to offer devotion, loyalty, and affection. Our faithfulness exists even in the face of hurtful acts. As we look at our relationship with our loved one, there may be some single act that requires forgiveness and a generosity of spirit that is hard for us to muster. There may be something that torments us and seems impossible to forgive.

If so, we can imagine placing this act along the continuum of our relationship with our loved one. We can view it only as an individual error along a broad horizon of favorable actions and deeds. We need not isolate or give undue importance to this single event. Doing so will only allow it to become disproportionate to the rest of the life events we shared with our loved one.

I will forgive with the same strength with which I grieve. As others have loved me and forgiven my unfortunate words or deeds, I too will forgive.

*It's so hard to break the habits I've grown used to—small
things we did together or for one another.*

Habit is not mere subjugation, it is a tender tie; when
one remembers habit it seems to have been happiness.

ELIZABETH BOWEN

The formation of habits is a natural outgrowth of any enduring relationship between two people. The habits can
be in the form of small gestures, endearing words, or private
routines. Whatever the habits are, they provide a sort of comfort. There is a predictability in the relationship when habits
are a part of it. Every time the habit is performed, it verifies the
bond between the two people. When one person dies and the
habitual word or act is missing, its absence creates a void. It
may be a phone call that came at a certain time of day or a
note, flowers, or other small gift we received on a regular basis.
Whatever it was, now that it is gone we feel a small, painful
stab when we notice that the habit we had grown so used to is
not there any longer and will never be experienced between
the two of us again.

When that happens we can remind ourselves that, by the
very nature of that kind of compatibility, we enjoyed a rare and
precious relationship. We can be sorry our loved one is not
there to perform the small habitual rituals that made up a portion of our life; but at the same time we will recognize the gift
of such a relationship. And we will benefit by talking about

this area of our loss to someone else, letting the other person whom we trust know what small things we miss most and why.

ᐤ *When I find myself startled and hurt by the absence of some familiar habit that made up a part of my life with my loved one, I will take a few moments to stop what I am doing and remember in every detail that gesture or word or the way he or she had of doing certain habitual things. And instead of keeping them to myself, I will share the memories of the things I miss most with someone else who knew my loved one.*

People tell me not to "dwell on it," to go on with my life.

Life is like music, it must be composed
by ear, feeling and instinct, not by rule.

SAMUEL BUTLER

*E*ach of our lives has its own rhythms. We need to be social at times and private at times. We need to give and receive affection at certain intervals. Similarly, our grief, which is part of our life, has its own rhythm. It is propelled by our feelings and our circumstances. The duration of its expression is guided by our instinct. To try to force grief into a time frame or a pattern will not work. Usually, within a reasonable length of time, we will have exhausted our need to grieve. Until such a time arrives, we will listen to the dictates of our own heart and not be troubled or offended by the uncomfortable urgings of others.

❧ *I will remember that others do not know me as well as I know myself. I will let my needs and instincts guide me as I focus on my loss and work through the feelings that dominate my thoughts and occupy my heart.*

I feel scared.

Behind everything we feel, there
is always a sense of fear.

UGO BETTI

*D*eath makes the world unpredictable. Isn't it now possible, we wonder, that *we* will die or get hurt or fail in what we do? We are sometimes afraid to do the things we did before the death. We may be afraid to drive, to go to public places, to take an elevator, or to cross a bridge. Fear goes hand in hand with vulnerability. And death makes us all feel vulnerable.

At times when our fear seems unmanageable, when it is restricting our daily lives, we need to recognize that it is a common response to death, but it is not a *necessary* response. We don't need to let fear dictate what we do or think. We can deal with fear by recognizing the other feelings that are linked to it, and by expressing and writing about each of those feelings.

We can write about our fear on paper, investigate it, and take it to its final conclusion. If we are afraid to return to our office after our loved one's death, what do we fear will happen? Will people avoid us? Or will they say something that will make us cry? And what if we do cry? Will there be any consequences? By writing about our fear, we remove its power. We put it in perspective.

 ࠳ *When I feel afraid, I will write down exactly what it is I fear. I will compare my greatest-fear scenario to what is most likely to occur.*

I feel as if I have to keep in motion. I find myself working overtime or running busily from one thing to another.

Rather abide at the center of your being;
for the more you leave it, the less you learn.

LAO TZU

*O*ne of the reactions we may experience during our grief is the need to keep in motion, to keep busy, to go from one thing to another, sometimes accomplishing very little. At the most extreme, grief may push us to hard-core workaholism, turning our job into a retreat from feelings, a place to plunge in and tackle a work-related problem instead of examining or experiencing grief-related reactions.

There's nothing harmful about this mode of behavior if it is temporary. At first, the escape may be saving us from emotional pain too difficult to bear, but eventually that escape must be abandoned so that the core feelings of our loss may be experienced. Again, until grief is expressed and fully experienced, it cannot be resolved.

So, after a brief period of time during which we engage in frenzied activity or hard, late hours at work, there needs to be a grounding, a time during which we can take a look at where we really are. Underneath all the time-consuming surface behavior, what is really going on? What motivations and conditions and disquieting thoughts invite examination?

≈ *I will slow down and allot time to take an emotional inventory. I will think about how I feel, what my needs are, what parts of myself I have been neglecting. I will not let the urge to be busy keep me away too long from the core of my feelings, where my grief will be resolved.*

Something needs to happen. I feel as if I'm flying apart—
one part going one way, one part another.

I don't want to locate myself only by geography (however strongly I acknowledge its power and point), or books, or beliefs. I want to be located in every breath I take.

PADMA PERERA

*A*s survivors, our space and time are disturbed. Our *place* in space and time is distorted when we are grieving. Sometimes we can't seem to "locate" ourselves. Our world is so chaotic and confusing it is difficult for us to focus, to get centered.

We can change these feelings of fragmentation and disorientation by taking a few minutes to "ground" ourselves. We can do this by using a simple stress reduction technique. First, we need to slow down, to sit quietly, close our eyes, and try to clear our minds of the thoughts that are dominating us at the moment. Then we can breathe in very slowly and deeply, hold the breath for a moment, and breathe out very, very slowly, making sure to expel the air in one long, steady, slow stream, not in starts and stops. Doing this breathing exercise just a few times will help us to calm our jumbled thoughts that have been bumping into one another, competing for our attention. The exercise allows us to focus on slowing our body's rhythm to a normal rate. It gives us time to become grounded so that we no longer feel as if we are segmented or scattered.

When I feel especially tense or disoriented, I will stop what I am doing, go into a room by myself, assume a comfortable sitting position, and perform deep breathing exercises. I will do this at least three times and as many as ten before I resume my other activities.

I can't get in touch with my feelings.

We hear "get in touch with your feelings" as if feelings
were external to our bodies. How could anything be a
more intimate part of ourselves?

ANONYMOUS

We hear a lot about the necessity for connecting with
our feelings, as if our feelings were in some other location rather than within us. Our feelings *are* ourselves. Every
important action we take is motivated by our feelings. These
may not be positive feelings; in fact, they may be quite negative. Some people's actions, for example, are so dictated by
their fears that they seem to have no other prominent emotions.

Regardless of which feelings we are experiencing, they are
what makes us human. As survivors we need to take time to
recognize what we feel, to sit quietly without outside distur-
bance and think about what is really going on beneath the surface of our daily lives. We can concentrate on recognizing the
feelings we have been experiencing since the death, for the
past hour, or simply for the moment. In this way we can "get in
touch" with core feelings that are the basis of our behavior and
our lives. We need to give these feelings air, to respect their existence, and to recognize their force.

❧ *My feelings do not exist outside myself like categorized com-
modities. They are within me every moment, with every breath I
take. I will not be so caught up in activity that I do not know what is
going on beneath the surface. I will allow myself the freedom to recognize what it is I am feeling. My feelings are what make me most
human. I will respect them.*

This grief is like a thing. It is a big, heavy, shapeless thing that is always there no matter what I'm doing or where I am.

If you continually grind a bar of
iron, you can make a needle of it.

CHINESE PROVERB

In our minds and hearts sometimes sorrow seems as if it is a huge, crude mass that weighs us down. Its very presence is disturbing because it seems so impenetrable and unmanageable.

But this mass of sorrow is no different from a bar of iron from which a needle can be made. We can work to diminish our grief each day, whittling away at the power of our unpleasant feelings and reactions by expressing and releasing them. Day by day, we can work toward getting this sorrow down to something manageable. We can watch our sorrow take on a shape that is not so crude, that has some definition, that seems to have some purpose.

∾ *I can work away at the mass of my grief, wearing it down little by little by releasing, relieving, and expressing all those components that make up my feelings of deep sadness and despair. Before long, the mass will be reduced in size. It will take shape as something manageable that I can continue to work with. I can make a needle of my sorrow to repair my life.*

I want things to return to normal, to be as they were before.

One cannot step twice into the same river,
for the water into which you first stepped has flowed on.

HERAKLEITOS

There is a tendency for us to long to return to the way things were before the death; yet we forget that the "normal" we knew, the life we had, cannot ever be the same normal. Our lives are fluid. Relationships are fluid. Everything about us is in constant motion. That is the nature of life; we cannot hope for our relationships to remain rocklike, without changing form, nor for our lives to be as photographs caught permanently for posterity.

Life is as a river. Even though we are stepping into the same river, we are not stepping into the same water, because the life we led before the death has flowed on. The life that is remaining is in motion, having been transformed by our loss.

❧ *The quality that makes my life alive is its fluidity, its change-ability. I know that what may once have seemed normal is now a state that has been washed away and replaced by another, which continues in constant motion. So I will reenter life after loss without the expectation that it will be much the same. I will be prepared to work toward readjustment and new understandings.*

I didn't think I'd ever have to go through something like this.

The act of dying is also one of the acts of life.
MARCUS AURELIUS

*E*xcept in cases where we wish our loved one to be released from pain or incapacity, death always comes too soon. For some survivors death is extremely premature: a young child dies because of illness, a teenager in an accident, a parent before even reaching middle age.

But still, the act of dying is truly one of the acts of life, for the moment we become mortal—the moment we are born—we are candidates for death.

Many cultures see death more as a part of life than we do in our Western societies. In fact, until it touches us personally, some of us see death as abnormal, an unfortunate event in someone else's life, but never our own.

It is difficult to incorporate the fact of death and its inevitability into our busy, demanding lives that are brimming with responsibilities, plans, and people. But we can help ourselves by recognizing that we are in the swing of a great arc which reaches from birth to death and that, at some point along that great invisible arc, we will begin the decline toward death, or we may even be among those who are swept down as swiftly as a falling star.

We know that death is what makes life precious. If we never died, life would be much less valued. All of this does not make the fact of our loved one's death less painful to bear. But it does help us recognize that although we may feel tortured and isolated by our experience or feel it is strange to go through such an experience, the grieving period can also be a time of transition for us, a time when we take stock of what we wish the bigger scope of our lives to be.

༉ *I will be incorporating my own and my loved one's mortality into what I think and do. This will help me gain appreciation for each phase of living and being in the world, each way in which I interact in my relationships and go about the business of my daily life.*

I see everything differently now.

Sorrows are our best educators. A [person]
can see further through a tear than a telescope.
LORD BYRON

*O*ne father commented that everything in his life changed
after his son's death: his job, his friends, where he lived,
his sexual drive, even his interests and goals. These kinds of
changes are not rare. Grief makes us view our lives differently,
rearrange our priorities, and cut out relationships with friends
who lack generosity of spirit in the face of our tragedy. Often
our lives become more sharply focused. There is a stronger
emphasis on feeling and less on acquiring.

We learn a great deal by going through grief. We become
more perceptive, more aware, more determined, and more ap-
preciative of traits we previously ignored in others. Most important, our vision expands to offer us alternative ways in
which to live our lives successfully.

☙ *I can acknowledge grief as a teacher, opening myself to new
avenues of thinking and feeling, being receptive to change and
growth.*

I don't want to hear anymore about time taking care of it.

You don't heal from the loss of a loved one because time passes;
you heal because of what you do with the time.

CAROL CRANDALL

*T*ime can do its work only if we help it. Just waiting for the passage of time after the death of a loved one is not enough. For example, a survivor could choose to begin drinking or to remain bound up in work to the extent that every emotion he or she had was being suppressed.

And we don't heal ourselves by being obsessive about activity, by sleeping away our lives, by dating twenty or thirty people, or by parking ourselves in front of the television set for a year or two. We heal by feeling what we need to feel when we need to feel it.

It can be helpful to spend time with others who are mourning the loss of our loved one, because we need to be in situations where we can experience the pleasure of recalling our relationship and sharing precious memories with one another. We can't just passively wait for ourselves to heal—or run away from ourselves in the hope that when we finally stop our frantic activity the grief-related feelings will have magically disappeared.

❧ *I will not expect to heal by running away from conditions, reactions, and emotions that arise as a result of this death. I will not remain passive and assume things will get better. I will put forth effort to make progress through this grieving process. This will include recalling, feeling, sharing, and memorializing my loved one. Today I will do one of those things; tomorrow I will do another. And I will continue on, day after day, until I know in my heart and mind that I have confronted the most difficult part of this sorrow.*

No, he's not suffering now. I'm the one who is suffering.

A man's dying is more the survivor's affair than his own.

THOMAS MANN

W̶e survivors cope with the death to a greater degree than the person who died, especially if the death was sudden. This causes some of us to feel resentment toward the person who died. It's as if the loved one took the easy way out and left us behind to cope, on a daily basis, with seemingly impossible issues.

It is only natural that here, on the other side of death, we may feel the need to recriminate. It's okay for us to do that. If we need to express our feelings of desertion, we can express them. If we find ourselves facing what appear to be insurmountable tasks and we wish our loved one were here to work with us to accomplish the tasks, we can talk about that. Having feelings that might be categorized as "negative" is permissible. It doesn't help to try to push such feelings away.

ᐤ *I know that surviving a death is a long, involved process. Some of the feelings I will experience, the thoughts I will think, and the wishes I will have will be dismal and repellent. Instead of being judgmental with myself about having such reactions, I will accept them as natural but temporary. I will discuss these feelings and any sense of guilt I may have about them with people whom I trust and within a supportive environment.*

There have been so many deaths in my life.

A man dies as many times as he loses a dear one.
SYRUS

*M*ost of the major events in our lives, our biggest challenges, are made easier if we have dealt with them before. But this is not necessarily so with death. If, for example, we lose a loved one early in our life and then another later on, the second death is not made easier by the first. In fact, it may be made more difficult if the first death has not been dealt with. Losses compound themselves, especially if they are not resolved.

That is why it is vital for us to work toward the successful resolution of our loved one's death. If we don't, the death will gain power over our life and hinder or damage it. The death can restrict us to the point of immobilization, or it can give rise to inappropriate or obsessive behavior, such as workaholism. As we take the necessary steps to confront and release our grief, we will progress toward our own health.

Even though we die a little with each death of a loved one, we must also live for the sake of continuing to care and to love.

❧ *I will give myself a chance to get beyond the invisible inner death I am experiencing after the actual death of my loved one. I will actively and persistently work toward the resolution of this painful loss, rather than stay immobilized in my own sorrow.*

Do you think it would be okay if I . . .

A question is usually a statement in disguise.

ANONYMOUS

*W*e have lots of questions about various facets of our grief. Is it okay just to leave his bedroom untouched for a while? Do you think she knew she was loved? Should I have stayed in his room a moment longer, or did he wait until I left the room to die? Will this pain ever end?

We often ask questions to which we instinctively know the answers. We may question our own behavior, the things we want to do, the way we feel about others, or the thoughts we have about death itself. Most often, the question we ask is really its own answer. For example, a survivor may ask: "Do you think it's all right for me to go to the cemetery and talk to him? It doesn't mean I'm crazy, does it?" The answers are inherent in the questions themselves: it is all right to go to the cemetery and talk to your loved one, and it doesn't mean you're crazy.

We ask our questions for reassurance. We ask to hear ourselves focus our concern. We ask so that we may have our opinions validated. We ask to clarify our thoughts, to bring them out into the open. But the majority of the time we already know the answers.

♻ *Many of the questions I ask come from a source deep within me, a source that can also supply the answer. When I have a particularly difficult question, I will trust that inherently I have the ability and the insight to know the answer. My questions are evidence of thoughtful conclusions that I have come to but have not yet voiced.*

Love hurts.

From love one can only escape at the price of life itself;
and no lessening of sorrow is worth exile
from that stream of all things human and divine.

FREYA STARK

Sometimes love hurts. And it hurts most when we are surviving the death of someone we love. It is at such a time that we look at ourselves and wonder what possesses us to love as strongly and as deeply as we do. Why can't we, we may wonder, love like other people seem to? Love and keep protected. Love ourselves to the exclusion of others. Love without having it affect the rest of our lives.

But such loves are not the kind of love we would truly value or benefit from. So we have to resign ourselves to being capable of love that hurts. To be otherwise would be to withdraw from life, to exist in a sort of emotional exile, not benefiting from or feeling *all* the joys of the human experience. Our love may be especially hurtful with our loved one gone, but the fact of that love is a gift.

ॐ *My love is hard to bear during this time of mourning, but I know that my ability to love with such intensity is a precious gift that all do not share. I will be thankful for that gift and will remind myself that it is my direct connection to all the most worthwhile aspects of my life.*

Maybe I love too deeply. I've been told I do.

The Eskimos had fifty-two names for snow because it was important to them: there ought to be as many for love.

MARGARET ATWOOD

When our loved one dies, that loss is the most important thing in the universe. We wonder why the world does not stand still at our loss. We notice, as we grieve, that love is not given as much importance in our culture as it deserves.

Love is not valued enough. On Valentine's Day, "love" is everywhere, in popular, accepted form. Then it disappears for the rest of the year. We may notice that around us love is linked with youth, and when we speak of our own particular love, some of the people in our lives find it embarrassing. Still others perceive our preoccupation with love to be a weakness, a flaw in our character.

But we can be grateful that we *have* love, that we understand that love lies at the core of any valuable relationship. It is the force that illuminates life, that distinguishes us from other animals and allows a special grace to enter our lives.

❧ *I will not fault myself or apologize for the depth and strength of my attachment to my loved one. I can reflect on that love with my support group and my friends, and not be embarrassed to discuss it. I will let it flow fully in my memories, and be thankful for loving and having been loved.*

Nothing around me even looks the same.

Despair is simply a harsh blindfold,
pulled over the eyes of hope.

STEVE TURNER

When we are first dealing with our loss, we look around us. Nothing we look at seems the same. Things we've seen all our lives take on a different shape, lose their color, recede into the distance. Flowers blooming next to a sidewalk may seem odd and out of place. It's as if everything that was once familiar and in its place is out of context. It doesn't fit. It doesn't add up. It doesn't appear to us as it should. We look at the world through the mask of despair, rather than through the eyes of hope.

Then, after a time, the colors around us brighten. The air seems clearer. Objects resume their proper size. The simple landscape of our lives—our streets, homes, neighborhoods, and stores—comes into clearer focus. The essential parts of our world begin to regain meaning, to stake their claim again in our daily existence. And it is the same with people whom we see when we are grieving. It's as if they are unimportant, even alien, to us. Then when we begin to feel better, our friends are once again our friends, our relatives come back into view, our co-workers take shape and form and are worthy of our attention. We join the world again.

❧ *My despair colors what I think and feel, what I see, and what I think I see. It influences what I choose to recognize and what I ignore. It makes me distant from the world I once was bound to. My despair acts as a harsh blindfold. I will remove that blindfold and look with new eyes at the worthwhile, the beautiful, the loving, the amusing things around me. I will let them into my life again so that I may be part of them as they are a part of me.*

I miss the way she made me feel about myself.

Ultimately, love is self-approval.

SONDRA RAY

When another person loves us, it affirms for us our worthiness. It makes us feel special. Being loved is being accepted, approved, cherished, and esteemed.

As a consequence, when our loved one dies, some of that self-approval drops away. Depending on our lives and the number of people whom we love and who love us, the impact of that change may be small, or it may be devastating. We may feel as if we are no longer important to anyone and that no one really needs or wants us.

∾ *By recognizing that I am suffering from a lack of self-approval, I can better cope with it. I can seek the support of others who care about me, though it will not be in the same way my loved one cared. I will nourish the bonds I have and be open to others. For it is by both giving and receiving that I can strike a balance and gradually fill in the void in my self that was made by the death of my loved one.*

Sometimes I wonder what she got from me.

You can give without loving, but
you cannot love without giving.

AMY CARMICHAEL

*O*ur loved one may have shown us love in ways that were different from our own. Now, upon reflection, we wonder if we ever showed love in the way that was important or necessary, or in a manner that was valued by our loved one. We may go over that question in our minds again and again.

But the answer is that we really cannot love without giving, and the ways in which we give may not be the same modes someone else would use to convey emotions. Our ways are uniquely ours. Our actions come from the heart. We must trust that even though we don't think we did enough, our expressions of devotion were understood by our loved one.

∾ *I recognize that it is not possible to love without giving, and that I gave. The manner in which I gave to my loved one was my own—an individual expression of my own character and personality. No two people express love in the same way. My way was the best way for me at the time. I know that my love was not invisible and that my loved one saw it and felt it.*

I don't think I can stand this emotional pain. It is too much for me to bear.

No emotion, no more than a wave, can
long retain its own individual form.

HENRY WARD BEECHER

The great surges of emotion that come as we cope with death often seem overwhelming. It's as if such strong emotions will surely drown us. Every part of us may be consumed by a powerful feeling that comes flooding in—often without warning. What can we do, we wonder, to escape such painful times?

We can remember that emotions truly are like waves. They wash over us, each time removing from us some of our sorrow, our despair, and our deep longing. They continue coming and coming until one day we find those painful feelings weakened, diluted, and no longer as engulfing.

༄ *Each time I cope with a surge of deep sadness, despair, yearning, or longing that overtakes my whole being, I will remember that it is that same wave that eventually will diminish my pain. The waves wash in and over me, but they do not drown me. Each wave of emotion is, in fact, healing me.*

Sometimes I feel as if my courage is all used up.

Courage is like an exquisite white cat coiled
against a bank of snow. When the creature
finally moves, there is a startling moment
of disbelief followed by delight and gratitude.

CAROL PASCOE

It takes a great deal of courage to get through grief—not the kind of courage that requires us to be brave and not show our feelings, but the type of courage that requires us to be brave and *experience* our feelings. During the grieving process, courage is that quality that won't allow our emotions to run and hide, that won't keep us from talking, that won't require us to "keep up a front."

Sometimes we feel as if we simply have no more courage, that we are tired of living through our grief and feeling our feelings and telling our stories. But that is because the fortitude that we think has deserted us is actually just coiled against the cold, colorless backdrop of our grief. It is always there even though at times its presence may be indiscernible.

❧ *I will have faith in my own courage, knowing that it is with me every day, waiting and merging in the background of all I do. Even when I don't see it stirring or don't believe it to be there, it has not deserted me.*

It seems as if there is so much more unhappiness to life than happiness.

Whole years of joy glide unperceived away,
while sorrow counts the minutes as they pass.
WILLIAM HAVARD

The positive experiences we had with our loved one, the most pleasant and loving memories, seem almost nonexistent compared to our suffering. In reality, there *were* good times, rewarding times, or loving times that we often experienced; but as we try to work our way through the feelings of loss after the death, our sorrow is so all-consuming it obliterates the past. Our grief slows time to a crawl and demands much of us, minute by minute and day by day.

Even though the sadness we feel makes our lives move painfully slowly, we need to have faith that as our grief begins to decline, we will accelerate our activities. We will reenter areas of our lives that we had temporarily ignored or abandoned. When we do, we will find that each day is not a test in agonizing endurance, but a regular day, with a beginning, a middle, and an end.

❧ *As I work my way through grief, my life will begin to resume its natural rhythm. The days and nights that are now made longer by sorrow will gradually assume their real length. I will make a space in my day to review the joyful times, the pleasant times, the times I shared with my loved one that provide me with nurturing memories.*

I don't understand what's going on with God.

God and the Devil were very far away. I used to pray, kneeling
at the open window. . . . now I seldom prayed . . . but still I
knelt at the open window looking and wondering.

JEAN RHYS

*I*t is hard to know where God is, why God allows certain
things to happen, if there is a God, where people go after
they die, if there is punishment or reward, or what happens to
us all. Some of us have firm convictions that guide us through.
Others of us have many questions that go unanswered. And
many of us go on "looking and wondering," just as Jean Rhys
did.

As one survivor put it, it hurts to be "disappointed by
God." All we can do to overcome this disappointment is to use
our human resources for coming as close as possible to understanding. We can accomplish this in several ways—by talking
with clergy, by reading for spiritual insight, or by discussing
our philosophical questions with members of our support
group. All of these serve as constructive steps away from despair and doubt.

❧ *I question God, as many do. Some of my beliefs have been
shattered. Instead of going over and over the same questions in my
mind, I will discuss them with someone who has similar concerns
and is qualified to offer guidance and help. Or I may choose to read
and explore spiritual or philosophical questions. Even though I need
to reconcile myself to the fact that I will never have all the answers I
wish to have, I will continue to work toward inner peace and understanding.*

I don't want people to talk to me about God. My loved one is dead, that's all I know.

Treat the other man's faith gently; it is all
he has to believe with. His mind was created
for his own thoughts, not yours or mine.

HENRY S. HASKINS

*A*s survivors, we may hear plenty about God. We not only hear the views of others, we may hear people questioning our own. We may hear explanations and expectations and deliberations that, unless they align with our own, are a real trial to listen to. In such situations we long for a way out. We don't know what to say or do. (We know what we would *like* to say or do, but we dare not do it.)

But it is important, even in the midst of discomfort or stress, to try to treat the other person's faith gently, to recognize that it is all that person has "to believe with." We do not have to listen if we don't want to, but we do not need to diminish the other person's faith. His or her thoughts may not coincide with ours, but that does not mean he or she doesn't have a right to think them.

❧ *When discussions arise in which I feel uncomfortable, I will withdraw from the situation quietly. I don't need to engage in a discussion I don't believe in, but I do need to remember that the other person's faith is all he or she has to believe with. He or she deserves to have the right to live within that faith, and I shall respect that right.*

I hate the way I have to live now. It makes me angry.

It is better to light a candle than to curse the darkness.
CHINESE PROVERB

We are alone and it hurts and makes us angry, but we do nothing to break the miserable cycle. We turn away from offers of help, friendship, and companionship to make our immediate world seem more bleak than it really is. Then we curse the darkness to which we've consigned ourselves.

We should, instead, create a spark for ourselves, do something to illuminate our long and difficult days. We need to make a conscious, determined effort to reach out and invite someone else into our lives, to create a welcoming atmosphere rather than one filled with anger and bitterness. After losing our loved one, we certainly have reasons to be angry and bitter, it is true, but we cannot let such feelings dominate our lives and further darken them.

❧ *I will think of myself as someone who can create light in my own darkness. I will do this today by responding to a friendly gesture, inviting someone to spend some time with me, making a phone call to someone I care about, or reaching out in a letter to a dear friend or loved one. I will neither amplify nor perpetuate the darkness in which I have been living.*

I got tired of trying to be everything I was supposed to be.
I became extremely depressed.

It isn't just being a good person that has made
me tired, but being any kind of person at all.

HARRIET JONES

For some survivors, grief does more than encompass sorrow and sadness; it produces deep depression. During this depression, life seems as if it is too much trouble. The smallest task appears to be insurmountable. Nothing interests us. We don't want to have to think or act—or even *be*.

Most of our reactions to loss we can work through. Some we can talk about or write about to get them focused and released. But this is not so with depression. Prolonged feelings of hopelessness cannot be ignored. When we suffer from such feelings, we need to seek the help of a professional, to have someone accompany us through the darkest of times, to give us some special skills for coping with our feelings—or even our total lack of feelings. Closing ourselves off when we are suffering from depression is destructive, and we must not do it.

✺ *If I do not feel myself getting better, if I am having difficulty maintaining a functional life pattern, if I have had severe sleeping difficulty for weeks or no appetite or lack of inspiration to do anything at all, I need to seek help. I cannot simply wait to get better. I need to recognize that I have gone beyond sorrow and sadness into depression and that I will benefit from having a professional person hear what I have to say and talk to me about the way I feel. I will do this not only for myself but for those around me.*

I feel so old.

How old would you be if you
didn't know how old you are?
SATCHELL PAIGE

Surviving a death makes everyone feel old. Young children who lose a parent feel old before their time. Parents who lose children feel older than their years. A person who loses his or her spouse ages upon the death. Just as being physically ill always makes us feel older than we are, emotional distress makes us feel the same way.

At first, this "instant aging" is something we live with. Then, after a while, the essential parts of our lives begin to fit back together. There seems to be a future, and we have the choice to be the age we want to be. We don't need to see ourselves as hopelessly aged before our time. Instead, we can choose to resume our life with the determination to generate personal energy that will buoy us up instead of weighing us down.

ॐ *Surviving the loss of my loved one has made me feel old and tired. Sometimes it makes me feel as if I am completely unable to do things I once did. But those feelings are unrealistic, and they are not helping me to heal. I am going to recognize that I have control over the age I act and the age I feel. I will begin deliberately infusing my life with renewed energy instead of giving in to the temptation to feel hopelessly old.*

Oh, it's too late in my life for that.

A child needs to make a sand castle even though
it makes no sense. In old age, with only a few
grains of sand, one has the greatest possibility.
SAMUEL BECKETT

*R*egardless of our ages, many survivors express the belief
that it is *too late*. Too late to change anything in our
lives, too late to try something, too late to express ourselves,
too late to reach out to someone we once knew and enjoyed.
Too late for any number of things.

But what does too late really mean? It may mean that a lot
of time has gone by since we first began thinking about making
a change or taking an action. It could mean that we have
no energy to do something. Or it might mean we don't believe
we are capable of producing a certain action, thought, piece of
work, or whatever.

To test whether or not we will and can do something, we
need to ask ourselves these questions: Do I honestly believe
that doing this will make a positive impact—regardless of how
small—on my own life or the life of someone else? Is it physically
possible for me to do it? Do I have a vision of what I want
this to be or do?

If we can answer these three questions, we will be able to
start working toward the change we are envisioning. We don't
have to wait around, as one survivor said, "until I get younger."

We can begin now by acknowledging our own power and possibility.

❧ *I will recognize that the possibilities in my life are put there by one person and that person is myself. By telling myself that it is too late to do something, I am really telling myself something else. If I truly want to do something, say something, cause some change in my life, I will look at exactly what I mean by "too late." Then I will develop a specific plan to combat those self-defeating limitations I have placed on myself. I will and can do the things that a false consciousness tells me it is "too late" to do.*

I want to give up.

Courage is like love; it must have hope for nourishment.
NAPOLEON BONAPARTE

Where do we get the hope we need to continue? When we feel as if we would like to give up and let our situation overtake us, how can we propel ourselves beyond that despair and resignation? The answer is that the very fact that we are experiencing our loss, that we are going through it rather than around it or over it, the very fact that we are not walking away from it and pretending that it isn't there, is one major reason to have hope. Because as we experience the depth of our feelings, as we examine our loss and all it means to us, we are working our way up and out of grief. We are coming into the light.

❧ *When all seems hopeless, I will remember that I am progressing through my grief, that I am processing the loss, that my most disturbing feelings can help me to work toward the resolution of the death. I have already had the courage to face my situation and to allow myself to be vulnerable. I will assure myself that this is the way through one of the most difficult times of my life and that, after a time, the pain will begin to ease. Through the days ahead, my sense of hope, now nearly an extinguished spark, will grow brighter and larger, and it will warm my life as it has the lives of countless other survivors before me.*

I get so tired of having to put on a front and say I'm okay when I'm not.

Be content to seem what you really are.
MARTIAL

When others ask us how we are, we're likely to respond with "fine, thank you," or something similar, even though we're experiencing deep sadness, longing, or despair. Regardless of our true feelings, we're conditioned to give a positive answer, and we often are so concerned about responding to the question in a polite, socially acceptable way that we don't reach out for support or companionship when we need it most.

When someone asks us how we are and we know that person is close enough or caring enough to lend us an ear or to help in some real, practical way, we need to let the person know how we feel. We can indicate that we're feeling lonely or sad, or that we're not sleeping well, or any number of other things. We don't have to try to hide our feelings or disguise our state of mind.

☙ *I know that there are people who would be supportive and helpful if only I would let down my social front and tell them how I'm really feeling. They need to have a signal from me in order to enter my circle of grief. So I will try to seem what I really am. By doing so, my exchanges with others will be more meaningful, and I will avail myself of more support.*

Being in public takes its toll.

When one is pretending, the entire body revolts.
ANAÏS NIN

$\mathcal{A}$s we attempt to return to our jobs or our social life, or just to leave the house to do errands, we may feel that we must hold our heads up and keep acting brave. So we talk about things that don't interest us instead of talking about what plagues our heart and mind. We reluctantly agree to do things in which we do not have the slightest bit of interest.

All of this takes a tremendous amount of energy. But it does something else, too. Our bodies are under a great deal of stress as we work through our loved one's death. Trying to create and maintain an artificial front contributes to that stress. And stress, of course, manifests itself in many ways throughout the body—in headaches, rashes, insomnia, digestive disturbances, the inability to concentrate, and the impulse to fidget or be on the move. We may also have more colds and flus as well as unexplained pains in various parts of our bodies.

One of the kindest things we can do for ourselves is to behave, as much as is possible and reasonable, in accordance with our deepest needs and desires. We can greatly reduce the amount of time and effort we put into doing what only seems socially required.

✆ *I will not push myself into false situations or require myself to perform in a way that differs significantly from my truest self. I will take care of myself by not forcing certain actions or responses, regardless of the pressure put on me to do so. My self, my body comes first, and I need to remember that my body will revolt against pretending.*

I don't like to lean on other people. They offer to help, but I don't want to bother them.

The hand that gives, gathers.
GERMAN PROVERB

*I*ndependence and self-reliance are fine qualities for us to have, but during grief we don't need to push those qualities to the forefront. It is more important to recognize what we need emotionally than to see how successfully we can suffer through alone. These are special times when we need to allow ourselves to accept help, to lean if we need to, to "bother" other people for simple forms of assistance.

If we feel self-conscious or hesitant about allowing others to help us, we can recognize that their help is not only a gift to us but, to some extent, a gift to themselves as well. It is a way for them to remove their feelings of helplessness when they see us mourning.

❧ *I will ask for and accept help when I need it most. If I need someone to talk to, to run an errand, or to give advice, I will ask. Rather than worrying about being a burden, I will remember that the person who helps is also receiving. I will remind myself: the hand that gives also gathers.*

I'm tired of people telling me to be brave. They don't know what this is like.

It is easy to be brave from a safe distance.
AESOP

*P*eople who mean well often say things that make us feel worse rather than better. For example, they urge us to be brave—to substitute bravery for grief. It is usually those who have little or no experience with having lost a loved one who will urge us to make courage our number one priority. They are giving us their advice at a safe distance from our experience.

It is not, in fact, a good idea to try to put bravery first when we are grieving. There is no law that says one must always be brave in life, no matter what happens. Sometimes our love is more important. Sometimes caring for others is more important. Sometimes holding back from something is more important. And sometimes grief is more important.

It is true that grief requires courage, but it requires it in conjunction with other behaviors. First of all, we must look after our own emotional needs. If we need to cry, then that is what we should do. If we need to ask for help or to talk about our loss, we need to do that, too.

Courage is needed to get us through the whole grieving process; but the kind of courage that overrides all else will only block out the rest of the necessary grief-related responses and conditions.

 When people tell me to be brave, I will remind myself that my first responsibility to myself is to grieve the loss of my loved one in any way that fits with my character and personality—as well as to indulge whatever reasonable inclinations I may have. I will listen to my own advice over the advice of those who have no experience in dealing with the death of a loved one.

I just want to be by myself and be quiet. I don't want to be where there is lots of talk or noise.

All profound things and emotions of things
are preceded and attended by Silence.

HERMAN MELVILLE

While working through our grief, we are likely to want to be quiet, to keep to ourselves much of the time, to mull over our innermost thoughts and desires and to avoid superficial conversation. This silent period enables us to explore ways we think and feel about the loss; it allows us to think about ourselves and what we need and wish and hope for. In a way this period of silence acts as a kind of restful absorption of our feelings and our energies.

It can serve, as well, as a period of growth during which we examine our relationship to our loved one, then center ourselves and determine how to go forward, how to emerge from our cocoon of sadness so that we may function in the world. This kind of productive and healing silence is important and acceptable.

At the same time, we need to recognize that silence that is prolonged, that becomes a way of life, is not good. Although we need to give ourselves time to be quiet and introspective, it would be unwise and unhealthy to let such a period go on indefinitely.

⚬ *My silence is a time for listening to myself, for enjoying calm, for centering on my innermost thoughts, needs, and desires. I will think of my silence as a meadow in my mind, where I can step out and enjoy the privacy and beauty it offers me.*

When I'm alone, I just keep reviewing the same things.

When one is alone, imperfection must
be endured every minute of the day.

FRANZ KAFKA

$\mathcal{S}$olitude has its benefits, but it also has its drawbacks. We can be plagued by thoughts that will not leave us alone, images we view over and over, conversations we keep rehearsing, or other painful thoughts and feelings that persist regardless of how hard we try to get rid of them. We question. We condemn ourselves. We condemn others. Everything that comes into our mind is a torment; yet we cannot shake free of our thoughts.

When we cannot rid ourselves of these speculations or self-criticisms and the like, we can weaken them by talking about them to someone else, preferably to a helping professional or a close, understanding friend who has also been through grief. If we feel that we cannot bring ourselves to talk about the thoughts that plague us, we can write them down in detail, describing our hurt, guilt, confusion, outrage, or whatever. The more detailed the description and the more power we give it on paper, the less power it will have to disturb us.

༚ *I will get rid of the sources of pain and anguish that come flooding in on me, particularly when I am alone. I will talk about them or write about them and by so doing will diminish their ability to dominate my thoughts.*

It's hard to explain. It's as if I'm ashamed of death.

I had what I see can go with total bereavement,
a sense of disfigurement, mortification, disgrace.
ELIZABETH BOWEN

*L*osing a loved one can sometimes cause us to have feelings of loss that are quite physical—as if there has been a severance of one part of the body from another. Death can also cause a sense of horror or create feelings of disgrace. Particularly in children, death causes one to feel ashamed and different.

Such feelings are too frequently reinforced by the society in which we live. Death provokes its own reactions in those around us, and those reactions, in turn, intensify our vulnerabilities and fears. We may feel feared by others, patronized, or shunned. But we need to recognize that even though death causes us indescribable hurt and makes us different from those who have not suffered a loss, we must not be ashamed of death. Eventually, it will touch the lives of all those who may be acting as if they are immune to it now.

❧ *While I may feel as if I have lost a physical part of myself, or I may be suffering from the stigma of death or feeling disgraced by death, I will recognize that these are unrealistic and temporary reactions. I will focus on myself as the whole, complete person I have been and will always be. The loss of my loved one has deeply affected me, it's true, but I will give myself time to heal, keeping faith in my return to wholeness.*

*I won't go to meetings or parties or even to the
gas station.*

Grief is a very antisocial state.
PENELOPE MORTIMER

A father remarked that before the death of his son he used
to leave his house to run errands a lot; he'd stop and
talk to his neighbor on the corner. He was involved in community affairs and attended lots of meetings. Once a week, he'd
enjoy going out to dinner with his wife. On the weekends, they
often went camping with other couples. But after the loss of his
child, his behavior changed. He didn't feel sociable at all. And
because his business was in his home, he found it easier to become reclusive. "I don't leave home now," he said, "unless I
have to. And most of the time I make sure I don't have to."

All survivors tend to avoid gatherings. We don't want to be
looked at. We don't want to have to hide our feelings. We don't
want to listen to conversations that seem inane. We don't want
to have to try to concentrate on something that doesn't interest
us in the slightest. Then, occasionally, we feel guilty about our
antisocial behavior. Or we wish we could change.

But grief *is* antisocial, and it's okay to pull away into our
individual privacies as we work toward resolving our loss.
Avoiding public gatherings is a natural reaction and one that
may last as long as a year. It is only when the grieving period
results in complete withdrawal—or prolonged withdrawal—

that we need to worry about ourselves, and then it would be wise to talk over our feelings with a helping professional.

    ❧ *I don't have to accept invitations from well-meaning friends if I don't want to. I can politely decline without feeling guilty. I don't have to make up excuses. I can just say I will be unable to attend. I have a right to withdraw for a period of time until I feel more comfortable being around others, have a higher energy level, and no longer fear being too vulnerable. But I understand that for the sake of my emotional health, this period of withdrawal must not be totally reclusive and must come to an end after a reasonable lapse of time.*

*I want to be with people, to let go of the hurt, but I think
I've forgotten how. It's been a year.*

Outside our private envelopes of pain, life lights
torches, sings songs, beckons with all its senses to
draw us out. We must eventually open: take part.

ESTEBAN ALVISO

*A*fter a period of painful isolation—which may have been
all-encompassing and prolonged—it is necessary to test
the waters in the world outside. This means venturing out at
least for a short time to watch or take part in some activity we
once enjoyed. Have dinner with a friend. See a movie. Go for a
long walk. Go somewhere to listen to music. Attend a sports
event. Visit the home of friends. Go window shopping. Attend
a lecture or concert. Seek affection. If we live alone, we can
begin by asking a friend to meet us for coffee and to talk so
that we can catch up on each other's lives. Even though we
may find it much easier to remain withdrawn, it's crucial for us
to try to venture out.

Emerging from our envelope of pain, even for a moment,
means risking our emotional safety and allowing ourselves to
be vulnerable. We may say we can't. We may say we don't want
to or we're afraid to risk it. We have been isolated for so long
that we don't remember the solid certainty of putting one step
after another, of trusting that we can set out and that we can
arrive. But we can do it. We might be a little unsteady, but
eventually we will become surer of ourselves and will benefit
from those things in life that beckon to us.

◡ *It has been a very long time since I have tried to go out, to talk
to people, to take part in any activity. I will now promise myself to*

venture out. I don't need to go someplace where it will be particularly difficult because of crowds or noise or social demands. I will pick something fairly simple that I have enjoyed doing in the past. I will schedule it now, marking it down and committing myself to do it.

I don't want to be around her. She doesn't understand at all.

Loneliness is to endure the presence
of one who does not understand.
ELBERT HUBBARD

We may be surprised by the lack of understanding shown by someone we had always considered to be one of our closest friends. We want desperately for that person to know how we feel, to give us the kind of verbal responses we need, to comfort us in the ways we value most. But, instead, this person in whom we had such faith seems not to understand us at all. This creates in us a loneliness—the loneliness that comes from facing something difficult without the help of the person we would choose as an ally, a supporter, a helper.

When this happens, we may make the situation worse by repeatedly trying to explain what it is we feel. (Or we grow weary of hoping the person will suddenly "catch on" to our grief.) We need to make the whole situation easier on ourselves by reducing our expectations when we see that person, by not trying to establish an emotional or psychological link. It wastes our energy. We need to surround ourselves with those who do understand even if they are only relatively recent acquaintances, such as those we meet in a survivors' support group.

I will drop my expectations that are not being fulfilled. I will not continue to set myself up by being in the presence of someone who does not understand what I am going through. Such experi-

ences only intensify my loneliness. I need to recognize when a person's capacity for understanding is not sufficient, and I should not waste my energy on trying to establish a connection. Later, when I feel better, I will look at this relationship and reevaluate it in light of what I have needed and what I have given and received.

I'm not the kind of person who tells my troubles to someone else.

Two in distress make sorrow less.

PROVERB

Sometimes we think that if we confide in someone else, if we tell the story of our loss, we are burdening the other person with our troubles or we are being too personal, too intimate. We fear that we will unveil too much about ourselves.

But during the period when we are working through our grief, it can be very valuable to have at least one other person in whom we can continually confide about what we are going through, what we are thinking, and what our fears are. There are hundreds of thoughts, feelings, conditions, questions, and assumptions that can be cleared up or lessened by talking them over with someone else, particularly with another person who has also experienced a loss.

We can help ourselves by accepting the companionship of someone—a friend or relative—who has reached out to us as we both mourn the same person. If we appreciate and enjoy the company of the other person, we can invite him or her into our life. We can call the other survivor and arrange to get together.

❧ *I will notice how I feel while I am with the person who has offered me friendship during my time of sorrow and how I feel after our visit. Do I get a sense of release and relief from being with the other person? Do I feel as if our grief is shared and that we feel better because of it? If I do, I will pursue the friendship and will offer whatever I can to make it nurturing for both of us.*

I wonder if this is the way I'll be treated for the rest of my life.

Why can't somebody give us a list of things
everybody thinks and nobody says, and another list
of things that everybody says and nobody thinks?

OLIVER WENDELL HOLMES

The social part of being a survivor is difficult. It would be so much easier if we had some sort of guide to get us through the confusing times when we're trying to sort out what someone says or see behind what someone says to what he or she really thinks or wants. We're talked to by some people in ways that seem irrelevant or insincere. We listen to claims of their devotion to us or of their understanding of our situation, but what they say lacks conviction. We want clarity and honesty and support. We don't want meaningless conversations that are composed of false messages.

These mixed social exchanges are the result of the lack of experience on the part of others and their general reluctance to confront the uncomfortable. In cultures where death is an accepted, expected part of life, there is less need for people to try to mask their feelings about death and about survivors' needs and situations. We can help ourselves by understanding this.

Once we have worked through the worst of our grief, we will be in a position to educate others regarding loss. When our personal energy merges with the correct opportunity, we may want to work to improve conditions for survivors within our community. This can be done most successfully through support services and grief-related organizations.

❧ *I recognize that other people feel at a loss to know what to do about the death I am surviving. They will say things they don't mean and mean things they don't say. I need to exercise tolerance and understanding when I feel neglected, hurt, or misunderstood. I will seek supportive companionship among my friends and relatives who have survived losses of their own. I will go where the understanding and support exist instead of complaining about the people around me who are unable to meet my needs.*

Sometime I'm going say exactly how I feel, and then the whole place is going to fall apart.

Our nervous system isn't just a fiction; it's a part of our physical body, and our soul . . . is inside us, like the teeth in our mouth. It can't be forever violated with impunity.

BORIS PASTERNAK

What Pasternak is saying is that our health will be adversely affected if we ignore our emotional needs. We cannot, for example, attempt to live in a way that does not correspond to our basic needs and desires. Such deceptions will harm us.

Our speech and thoughts and feelings are not one thing and our physical body another. They are all part of a whole. We need to have enough respect and concern for ourselves to value our own emotional core. This is exceptionally important when we grieve, because our physical condition has really been weakened by grief. We can weaken it further by not being true to ourselves.

➳ *To keep healthy, I need to do more than eat and sleep and get some exercise. I need also to recognize that emotions that are covered over, and conditions that are lied about, erode my physical well-being. I will not put that extra stress on myself.*

I used to be good at making decisions. Now I can't decide which way to turn when I get to the end of the block.

Some of his decisions were accurate.
A stopped watch is right twice a day.
ANONYMOUS

Surviving a death seems to wipe out many of our capabilities; one of them is making decisions. A widower complained that deciding whether to make decaffeinated or regular coffee in the morning took him twenty minutes. Other survivors have been disturbed because their impaired decision-making ability caused them difficulties at work.

Being unable to make decisions is a natural aspect of the grieving process. As survivors, we are dealing with an underlying and constant distraction of the greatest magnitude. Though we may try to function well on the surface, the great pull of sorrow saps our mental energy. We easily lose our train of thought, are too tired to think through a process or procedure, or fail to remember something we have just been told or shown.

For that reason, it is extremely important for us not to make any major changes in our lives when we are grieving. We should not plan to move, get a divorce, change jobs, get married, adopt a child, or sell a treasured possession. If at all possible, all decisions of importance should be put on hold until at least a year after the death.

❧ *I will not make any major decisions for the first year, unless doing so is absolutely unavoidable. And I will not worry about my inability to make lesser decisions. It may take me longer than I expect, but it is all part of the grieving process. My uncertainty and instability are only temporary.*

I can't see something that isn't. I can only see things the way they are.

Suppose someone were to say, "Imagine this
butterfly exactly as it is, but ugly instead of beautiful."
LUDWIG WITTGENSTEIN

When people try to cheer us up, when they ask us to think of our lives in ways that seem impossible, it's as if they are saying, "Imagine your life exactly as it is, but totally different." Their encouraging visions and predictions regarding our days ahead (which will have—they promise us—serenity and normalcy and any number of positive qualities) are beyond the scope of our imagining. We don't get what they're telling us. We don't even *want* to get it. Because, in the grief-stricken world we're in, we think there is no room for such a positive picture.

The survivor who offered the above Wittgenstein quote remarked that her own life after the loss of her son was comparable to the ugly butterfly. "When you're in it and experiencing it as the ugly butterfly, it's almost impossible to imagine the butterfly as it is." In other words, it was hard for her to imagine the true nature of her life, her life before things were turned upside down.

∾ *Each day that represents the dark side has as its opposite the beautiful side. Even though it may seem unavailable to me now, that doesn't mean it isn't there. I will strive to create a vision for my own life that projects the best rather than the worst. I will hold that picture in my mind for a certain length of time every day until I begin to see it without trying.*

He hasn't made any real effort to get together.

One of these days is none of these days.
GERMAN PROVERB

*I*f a friend says, "We have to get together one of these days," and we know he or she doesn't mean it, it's hard for us not to feel offended. We sense that getting together with us is not a top priority for our friend, yet we thought he or she valued our friendship. This happens frequently with widows and widowers whose former friends treat them differently when they're no longer a couple. It happens to parents who have lost a child and who feel as if they're making other parents uncomfortable.

We have to acknowledge, however reluctantly, that some people cannot bear to be even minimally exposed to death and grief. It doesn't mean they don't like us or don't care what happens to us. They may care a great deal but not be capable of expressing it because of circumstances (or a past history) of their own. Some friends cannot even attend a funeral. It is important to recognize that, through no fault of their own, some people cannot cope with emotionally demanding situations. When we feel avoided or put on hold, we can focus our energy on those friends who do come through, who make an effort to spend quality time with us.

❧ *I will not expend energy being angry or hurt by someone who is unable to interact with me. I know grief is not a disease: it is part of life, and I will be thankful for the mature and concerned friends I have who recognize my needs and who are able to show me they care.*

*I don't want to be patient! I want to do something
to change the way I feel.*

Patience is not passive: on the contrary,
it is active; it is concentrated strength.
E. G. BULWER-LYTTON

*B*y forcing ourselves to be patient, we *are* doing something. We are exhibiting the strength it takes to get through this challenging and changing time of our lives. The kind of strength that gets us through our grief does not consist of smiling and keeping our chin up. It is, instead, the kind of strength that says, among other things: "I'll wait this out. I'll recognize that grieving takes an inordinate amount of time. No matter how many times I have to relive the same emotions or be plagued by the same feelings of devastation, inadequacy, or fear, I recognize that it is all part of the process. I need only to persevere and have faith that there is an end to that process. Having patience is having power."

∾ *Even though it seems as if I should be changing faster, I will be patient and recognize that grief requires that I wait. Having patience with particularly difficult feelings or conditions gives me the power to get through them gradually as I need to. Eventually, I will be able to emerge from this emotional turbulence. I will keep in mind now that if I become impatient or angry or demand change when it is not possible, I am only delaying my healing process.*

I'm tired of some people telling me they know how I feel
when they don't have the slightest idea how I feel.

A polite man is one who listens with interest to
things he knows all about, when they are told
him by a person who knows nothing about them.

DE MORNY

It requires great restraint for us to have a conversation with someone who professes to understand the intensity of our grief but actually has no personal experience with surviving a death and, as a result, knows relatively little about it. Such a person is often well intentioned but sadly lacking in the ability to truly empathize with us.

What can we do if we find ourselves in such circumstances? If the conversation is a one-time event or the speech that begins with "I know exactly how you feel" is one we're only going to have to hear once, then we can give polite attention to the speaker and say nothing in reply. But if this type of conversation happens more than once with the same person or becomes part of a regular pattern of behavior, then it is best to say something calmly but firmly to end the false empathy once and for all: "I know you think you know how I feel, but the truth is I am the only one who knows exactly how I feel, and it really makes things worse when we have these conversations—so let's talk about something else for now."

I will be polite to other people, but I will not become trapped as a regular listener to someone whose remarks are more hurtful than helpful. I will say what I am feeling and put an end to the conversations that offer me advice or opinions that are not appropriate for my situation.

When I see the two of them together, I feel so envious.

To envy another's situation is only a way that
we compare our insides to others' outsides.

STEPHANIE ERICSSON

We experience the pangs of envy that come from watching other people whose relationship was the same as our own—husband with wife, friend with friend, sister with brother, father with daughter. We look and we watch and we wish. We think how lucky the other two people are, and we feel suddenly stricken by a renewed load of sadness. We would give anything to have our loved one back, to be interacting as the others are, to be relishing our relationship instead of taking it for granted as we often did.

As we observe others and envy them, we imagine that their lives are painless, that they have what they want, that their challenges are less than ours. We think we have been punished and robbed while they have not. It is terrible to have to watch them. We are sure they are unaware of the value of the relationship they are privileged to have.

But we don't know what others' true relationships are by looking at them. If we watch a mother buying her daughter a toy, or a wife taking her husband's hand as they enter a movie, or two friends hugging in greeting on the street, we don't know what misfortunes have entered their lives or will enter their lives to challenge them as we have been challenged. We can't assume that it is only our own lives that have been touched by difficulties while others' around us go on successfully and without trial.

꙰ *I ache when I see others together. I envy them so much. When that happens next time, I will tell myself that I am only "comparing my insides with others' outsides" and that I have no right to want to subtract from their lives anything that I wish to add to mine. We all have our own challenges and losses and disappointments, and for the most part they don't show. I will put my envy in its proper perspective. Perhaps one day I will even be able to be happy about the loving relationships shared by others.*

I know I could have been a better father (or mother, son, daughter, friend, or lover).

To dream of the person you would like
to be is to waste the person you are.

*A*fter the death of a loved one, survivors often punish themselves with self-blame for not having been a perfect partner in the relationship that is now gone forever. But just as it is inadvisable to make major life changes during the grieving process, it is also unwise during this difficult time to try to make ourselves over to become the more perfect person our guilt tells us we should have been.

Grief can certainly yield valuable personal insights and changes, but these will naturally mature as our lives evolve when the grieving process diminishes. We only delay that desired outcome when we direct our energies to wishing we were something that we never can be or quickly attempt to redesign ourselves—the way we dress, talk, work, or interact with others—like some character in a play.

We can promise ourselves to work to be a better person as we make our way out of grieving and back into a more normal daily life. But making ourselves whole, and completing that journey, is our first task. And to do that we must accept ourselves, avoid blaming ourselves for the past, and recognize that guilt is not a good basis for making changes. We cannot wish away the life we have or the person we are.

ᴥ *I will not devote my time to impossible fantasies—fantasies that arise from dreaming of the person I would like to be. Doing so wastes the person I am. I will concentrate my time and energy on the person I know myself to be. I can make a deal with myself that I can work toward self-improvement, toward reaching my maximum potential, but I won't waste the person I am in the process.*

I feel as if I want to cry, but I don't do it.

Tearless grief bleeds inwardly.

C. N. BOVEE

*S*ometimes a survivor will say he or she is unable to cry. And other survivors say crying doesn't solve anything or bring anyone back. In fact, quite a case can be argued against crying, especially by those who feel their greatest accomplishment after a death is masking their feelings. But holding in tears and suppressing sadness can produce negative effects. And those effects may not always be visible.

A study that was done with two groups of babies, those who were able to cry tears and those unable to cry tears (because of a congenital abnormality), found that the latter group had a significantly higher stress level. With adults, it was found that the tears we cry when we are sad have a different chemical makeup from the tears we cry when we are not sad, for example, when we are peeling an onion. Crying from sadness actually gets rid of debilitating toxins in the body. When people say, "I feel better after a good cry," the statement should be taken literally. When we have the impulse to cry but think we shouldn't, we must not fight back our tears; we need, instead, to let them come.

❧ *Crying is nature's way of releasing my stress and helping me heal. No one has been harmed by crying, but people have been harmed by suppressing their emotions and stifling their tears.*

Once I began crying, I could not stop.

The emotions may be endless. The more we
express them, the more we may have to express.

E. M. FORSTER

*O*nce we unleash our emotions, we may be surprised by
their depth and their intensity, but we will not be hurt
by expressing them. We may cry until we think we can cry no
more—and then start over again.

There is a well of feelings that resides in each of us following a death, and we must dip down into that well and pull and
pull until everything has been pulled to the surface. Even
though it may seem as if there is no end to our grief-related
feelings, they will, one day, exhaust themselves and be replaced with other feelings that are less burdensome to deal
with. Eventually, the very hardest parts of grief will have been
lived through and integrated into our lives. Until then, we
should not fear our own tears. We can think of them as agents
we can depend on to remove the sadness from within us.

∾ *When I have feelings of deep sadness and bouts of crying, I
must recognize that what seems to go on forever is not really endless. By unleashing the feelings that cause me to cry, I am helping
them to gradually dissipate, to lose their power. I am setting them
free so that I, too, may one day be released from grief's torment.*

I take it [grief] everywhere I go.

Some heard or saw nothing, but felt again that pang,
nameless and centered below the throat,
of sorrow which had become . . . like an organ in their flesh.

LOUISE BOGAN

*O*ur grief may seem sometimes as if it were a real live animal thing that has taken hold of us. We have learned to make room for it inside ourselves, and it travels with us wherever we go.

What do we do about it, then? Is there anything we can do? The answer is yes. We can ease the weight of this sorrow by always permitting it an escape. As we let it out through talking with friends or relatives, talking to ourselves or to our loved one at the cemetery, writing about it, or sharing in a support group, this grief will gradually dissipate. For now, we can exercise our power as we choose which part of our sorrow to share, which part to give away, and which part to keep to ourselves until later. Eventually, little by little, we know we will need to let it go. All of it.

❧ *When I feel the heaviness of sorrow inside of me, I will remember that I have power over it. I know how to do the things that bring relief and release. Even if I work at the release a little at a time, with only a few people, or in only one or two situations, I am still unburdening myself. I will not hoard my sorrow and require my body to bear a load that is more than it should bear.*

*I used to think of myself as strong. Now I'm so weak
I can't believe it.*

There are two kinds of weakness: that which
breaks and that which bends.

JAMES RUSSELL LOWELL

*O*ur courage is tested every day of our grieving period. We
gather strength—not to mask grief or to ignore it, but to
express it. What we may consider to be weakness can actually
be strength. In these days that try our spirit, our minds, and
our bodies, we don't fold up. We lean, we bend, we rearrange,
we figure out another approach, we soften—but we don't
break.

What we may see as our weakness is our innate ability to
survive in a wide variety of ways. To bend is not to succumb or
to collapse, it is to accommodate the feelings and responses of
grief, to figure out how to live with them.

❧ *I am not weak because I bend. I bend to keep from breaking,
and it is in the bending that I learn to accommodate the strongest responses of grief. I do what I need to do to get through this time, and I
do it with a view toward wholeness, not fragmentation.*

I'm trying to stay strong for everyone else, but it's hard.

We are all here on earth to help others; what
on earth the others are here for I don't know.

W. H. AUDEN

*T*his quote reflects the exasperation experienced by some survivors who find themselves having to take responsibility for everything. And during the mourning period there are a multitude of things to look after. In addition, for most of us, there are other survivors for whom we feel responsible—either totally or partially. Some of us become so involved in trying to assume all the responsibilities and attempting to meet the needs of other survivors that we shove our own needs and desires into the background. In fact, sometimes they are so successfully pushed away that we don't even know what they are. Then, one day, we realize we've been supporting everyone else and that we're burning out fast.

At such a time, we need to step outside the circle in which we function most of the time. We need to stand back and survey all that we have been doing, take note of what others have been doing, and consider who and what has been getting the most attention and why. We need to rearrange our schedule and modify our behavior so that we are not always in the position of serving or helping. We need to make it possible for others to assist us.

ॐ *I am capable and giving, but I have overused both of these qualities—to my own detriment. I need to take a break from being a constant caregiver and manager so that other survivors can develop their own coping skills and take responsibility for their own personal progress. I am not being uncaring by doing this. I am giving myself a chance to pay attention to my own needs and to revitalize my energies.*

*I think I'll just detach myself from the whole scene
if I can.*

To spare oneself from grief at all cost can be achieved
only at the price of total detachment, which excludes
the ability to experience happiness.

ERICH FROMM

We may yearn to have our feelings dulled, to be free from deep longing for our loved one who died. We miss him or her so terribly, and we want, once more, to be able to express our love, to hold, to be with. These feelings are powerful and override everything else we try to say and do. We long for escape from them. We want to distance ourselves. We wonder why we have to bear such hurt, such emotional agony.

But the only alternative to never grieving is never having established a close, loving, and happy relationship with anyone. If we have a strong, fulfilling relationship in our lives, then we are eventually going to experience grief. We should remind ourselves that our deep feelings of loss are only evidence of our ability to care truly for another and to enjoy life with another—and we would be lonely, unhappy souls without such a capacity.

ᖙ *When I am questioning why I have to feel so deeply, when I am wishing that I didn't have such a capacity for emotional pain, I need to remind myself of the alternative. If I had never had a loving relationship that gave me happiness, I would not now have these feelings of torment. I wouldn't give up the vastly rewarding life experience I had with my loved one to avoid the grieving experience after my loved one's death.*

I want to talk about him all the time, but I don't want to make others feel sad.

He has not lived that lives not after Death.
ENGLISH PROVERB

We may want to talk about our loved one frequently; in fact, we may fear that our need to talk is excessive. But talking about a loved one who died is a testament to that person's life. It is a reflection of all that person offered to us and to others. It signifies that our loved one had a unique personality and character and was a strong influence in our lives, that he or she gave something valuable to us and received from us as well. Talking keeps the person alive in important ways. It confirms that our loved one will be an ongoing part of our lives and the lives of those around us, that he or she came into this world and had an impact, and shall live in our hearts and minds forever.

   I recognize that it is okay to talk about my loved one, to review my loved one's life, to tell stories, and to recount special memories. Talking keeps my loved one's memory alive. To keep quiet and pretend he or she didn't exist would be to deny a valued loving relationship and the unique role that person played in my life as well as in our community of friends and family.

I've never been very brave.

Courage is fear holding on a minute longer.
GEORGE S. PATTON

We think of fear as one thing and courage as another. In reality, they are related. But when we slip from the territory of fear into the powerful realm of courage, it occurs so naturally we do not think about it. The same fear that makes us shrink inside ourselves also charges us with the necessary force to move forward into the face of threat and serves as a catalyst for our bravery.

Grief continually presents us with all kinds of reasons to be afraid. As survivors we face situations now that we could never have anticipated, and we often have to deal with them alone, unaided. We have to meet those situations with a mind, body, and heart that have been wounded. But whenever we feel especially afraid and do not think we can withstand the feeling, we can tell ourselves that holding on a minute longer will make the difference between caving in and having power over the situation.

ॐ *Sometimes I feel as if I cannot find the bravery I need to work through grief. But I will tell myself, when fear threatens to debilitate me, that I will hold on a minute longer and turn my fear into courage.*

When will this be over?

We are tomorrow's past.
MARY WEBB

We don't realize it, but when we are going through grief, each day we move toward resolution of our loss. Each day that we grieve, that we deal with painful feelings, is another day that we can add to the passage of our grief.

It does take time. But during the process we don't ignore, turn away, or minimize feelings that want expression. We relive conversations and events if we need to. We express regrets or yearnings. We seek the support of others. And all the while we do not torment ourselves with the length of our grieving process; we do not constantly question when it will be over, when it will end. We don't ask ourselves, another week? another month? the rest of the year? We just add one day at a time to our "past grief." When grief finally loses its power over us, when it begins to diminish, it will have happened so gradually we may not recognize it.

ᐧ *For now, I will remember that I am acting each day as I need to and that when tomorrow comes, today will have become a portion of the grief that is behind me. Each day brings me one step closer to resolution of my loss and a permanent easing of my pain.*

I can't accomplish what I want to accomplish anyway.
It's too late.

Life is short, but it's wide.
SPANISH PROVERB

Surviving a death puts us in touch with our own mortality. Life, as we view it now, may seem unbearably short, like a small interlude that barely gives us time to do and be. This brevity is underscored when our loved one's life is shorter than average or shorter than we or anyone around us expected.

As we look at our own lives, we need to see them as a time to be lived to the fullest, regardless of the number of years involved. Our lives may not be long enough in duration, but it is up to us to make them wide enough. We can now reinvest our energies, make our plans, carry out our actions, explore, help, create, learn, grow, and delight in earthly things. We can make our lives rich, wondrous experiences. We can reach out to those who follow us on their own course of grief. We can *be* alive in many ways, rather than just staying alive after our loved one's death.

∾ *I do not control the length of my life, but I control its width. My life will encompass a wide variety of worthwhile, enriching experiences and actions. And throughout the rest of my life I will be constantly aware that one of the most rewarding aspects of being alive can be to assist others, to broaden the scope of personal caring and compassion.*

I found something inside me that I didn't know I had.

That which does not kill me makes me stronger.
FRIEDRICH NIETZSCHE

This tragedy, we think, will kill us. Then as we struggle to keep ourselves going and to meet the challenge, we learn something about ourselves. We find that we have a reservoir of strength that has remained untapped up to this point in our lives. We are surprised by our own ability to persevere, to get up again and again and struggle against the flow of great sadness. We may even find ourselves helping others who grieve, without realizing we had such capabilities. We thought we were too far down and too incapacitated to try to assist anyone. Then there we were, doing what we didn't think we could ever do. The tragedy is not killing us, we learn, it is making us stronger.

☙ *When I feel I cannot go on, when I feel that no one could go on in such circumstances, I will remember that people often have more strength than they realize they have. I will reach down deep inside myself and tap that core of strength that has brought me this far, and I will know that it can take me the whole distance.*

Don't expect me to be over it.

Tears may be dried up, but the heart—never.
MARGUERITE DE VALOIS

For most of us, right after the death our tears are on the surface. Then, gradually, our emotions seem less raw. We are able to get through a whole day once in a while without feeling ourselves give way to grief. At this point we might worry that something is wrong with our devotion. We may wonder if fewer eruptions of grief mean that we no longer love, that we no longer care.

This is, of course, not true. The intensity of our grief is significant when we are working toward resolution of the loss, but the duration of our grief is less important. The length of the grieving process does not measure the strength of our love. We do not need to grieve longer because we love more. When our tears have dried up, it does not mean our heart has grown cold. It only means that we have worked our way through the worst of times. The love we have for our loved one is still steadfast in our hearts.

ᘓ *I will not equate the length of my grieving period with the degree of my love. One has nothing to do with the other. I will cry until I no longer need to cry, will grieve until I no longer need to grieve. And through it all, my love will continue unchanged and undiminished.*

Five months after the death, we had a private ceremony, just a few of us. It helped a lot.

Ceremony is really a protection, too, in times of
emotional involvement, particularly at death.

AMY VANDERBILT

We are all familiar with the necessary ceremony at death. The time and location of the funeral service are among the first things people want to know after hearing of a loss. But there is another kind of ceremony that many survivors have found to be enormously helpful as they yearn for their loved one, and that is a special ceremony that is conducted out of choice. Such a gathering is planned by a few close members of the family or a small group of friends to serve as a very personal way of honoring their loved one in an intimate and private good-bye. Some people choose to create a ceremony on the anniversary of their loved one's death, some on the loved one's birthday, and others just select a time that is mutually appealing to those who will participate.

The ways of honoring our loved one's life are as many as there are people. Finding the way that seems most appropriate for our situation can be a task that brings together a select group of survivors and strengthens the bond that already exists among them.

❧ *I can plan a private ceremony to honor my loved one. It will be a time for the survivors who were closest to my loved one to celebrate his or her life, share meaningful memories and photographs, and talk about how our loved one contributed to our lives.*

Just because I've said good-bye doesn't mean I'm used to it.

A thousand goodbyes come after death—
the first six months of bereavement.
ALAN GREGG

When someone we love dies, we don't say good-bye just once. We say it over and over. And we don't just *say* good-bye, we *live* good-bye. That is, we continually have to distance ourselves from the daily bond we shared with our loved one and detach from the expectations we had in our lives because of that bond.

Saying good-bye helps us to understand the reality of our loss, because even though the reality is with us one moment, it may not be the next. So we can say good-bye in any way that feels right to us. We may talk to our loved one's photograph. We may have a weekly—or even daily—conversation at the cemetery. We may write our loved one a letter saying all the things we wish we could have said aloud. We can talk with our support group about the difficulty of letting go. Or we may decide to have a private ceremony in which we release our loved one. We allow ourselves as many ways of acknowledging death as possible.

✺ *I will accept that I'll need to say many good-byes, especially during the first six months after my loved one dies. During this period of time when I am struggling with the reality of separation, I will do whatever I can to acknowledge the finality of my loved one's death. And I will be patient with myself, knowing that it takes a great deal of time to believe something I do not wish to believe.*

I don't have any confidence anymore. I don't feel I'm worth anything.

Every new adjustment is a crisis in self-esteem.

ERIC HOFFER

*D*eath shakes all of our foundations. One of those foundations is our self-esteem. Now, when we suffer from feelings of worthlessness, we must remember that we have had confidence in the past, that during that time other people saw us as a desirable, capable, talented, or attractive friend, co-worker, companion, or lover. We are still that person. We still have all the good qualities that make others see us as an appealing and worthwhile person.

It's true that our self-presentation might have taken a beating because of the death. We have been tested. We have been dulled. But our specialness is still there in us. We need to remember that this crisis in our self-esteem is only temporary. As we begin to experience sorrow less, we will be able to allow our strong personal qualities to come to the surface, to be exhibited more, to give us a sense of belonging, once again, among those who are confident.

I am just as capable as I once was, just as appealing, just as important to those around me. I must not sell myself short or give up on myself in tough situations. I must not think that I am unworthy of attention, love, or reward. I am as much a worthwhile person in the eyes of myself and others as I ever was. I have a lot to offer this world I live in.

I can't quit questioning—why did she die?

There are two ways to slide easily through life:
to believe everything or to doubt everything;
both ways save us from thinking.

ALFRED KORZYBSKI

*D*eath leaves us with many questions. We may ask why our loved one died. We may question religion in general, God's intentions in particular, the reason for an early death or a violent death, or why our loved one had to endure a prolonged period of pain. Such thoughts and questions may plague us on a daily basis, defying resolution. We feel tormented by the fact that we don't seem to get anywhere in our quest for answers, that no one we consult can be definite. There is no reassurance that our questions are legitimate, no proof that our conclusions—if we reach them—are right or wrong.

Most of us can neither believe nor disbelieve everything throughout this life, so we question. We concern ourselves with understanding and knowing. It's a sign that we are curious, thoughtful individuals. It is okay to question. It is okay to doubt; it is part of our life experience. We may benefit in this search for understanding by having a trusted confidante accompany us. We can open up our doubts and questions by sharing them with a trusted friend, our support group, or a helping professional. Sometimes discussing with someone else those questions that occupy our thoughts can make our quest less lonely. But we must realize that for some of our most agonizing questions, such as "Why did she have to die?" there really are no answers.

❧ *Some of the most profound questions can only be explored and discussed. As I put effort into doing this, I may bring up various issues with someone whose opinion and experience I respect so that I can have a sounding board. But as I grapple with the hardest of questions, I will acknowledge that some of them have no definitive answers. I will, in time, need to replace my obsessive questioning with acceptance.*

How do I know there is anything beyond this life?

Doubt makes the mountain which faith can move.

PROVERB

*S*ome survivors confide that sometime during their life they made an unusual agreement with their loved one. The agreement was arrived at after the two had discussed life after death, after they had talked together about what may exist beyond life on earth. The agreement made between them usually was something like this: the one who goes first is supposed to come back if it's possible (in a dream or in some other way) and explain what death is and if there is life after death.

Many of us are annoyed and tormented by our own doubt. As we consider questions of life after death, reward or punishment, reincarnation, or a multitude of spiritual questions and concerns, the mountain of doubt gets bigger and bigger and more and more difficult to climb.

When this happens, we must recognize that the expectation of being able to have firm knowledge about what happens after death is unreasonable. We can take as our solace what, with our loved one, we believed about death, and life after death. We can remember what the two of us hoped to be true, what made us both feel assured and strong and purposeful. These are the components that make up our faith—the kind of faith that is bigger than doubt, that can move the mountain of doubt.

❧ *I acknowledge that in moments of deep sorrow it is difficult to give credence to God or any other deity, or to a spirit or power I might once have believed in, but I will try. I will recall the faith my* loved one and I created between us to carry us through the most difficult times. It was a faith that constructed its own peacefulness. Allowing a similar peacefulness within myself now makes it possible to imagine it elsewhere.

*I've always known how important it was to love someone.
But now I understand love's value in many new ways.*

That is what learning is. You suddenly
understand something you've understood
all your life, but in a new way.

DORIS LESSING

One of the first impacts grief has on us is to illuminate our lives in ways we had never anticipated. Often, one of the results of that illumination is to see with new eyes the scope, depth, and power of our love as well as to recognize fully the necessity for receiving love in our daily lives.

If we think we didn't recognize the depth of our love before the death occurred or if we think we didn't express love fully enough, this assessment can cause us great remorse. It can also cause yearning and regret if we believe our love came too late in the relationship.

We review our bond with our loved one and try to repaint the picture the way we want it to be. We may even be angry at ourselves. But such anger can only be replaced with forgiveness and the determination to allow love to enter our lives, to take its prominent place in our present and future relationships. We come to it now with a deeper perspective and perhaps a new capacity for commitment—whether it be to love a child, a spouse, a friend, a sibling, or a lover.

༄ *I have always understood the need for love in my life, but the death has made me understand it in a new way. I will not punish myself for any inadequacies—imagined or otherwise. Instead, I will apply what I have learned about love to the other close relationships I have now and to those new ones I will have in the future. Love will be a major factor in reshaping my life.*

I want to contact her and see if she needs company or wants to talk, but maybe I should wait awhile.

He who waits to do a great deal of
good at once will never do anything.

SAMUEL JOHNSON

*T*here may be another survivor whom we believe could benefit from some communication with us. We have every good intention of making a call, but we keep delaying it, because we think we'll have more to offer later on. And this may be true.

Right now, immersed in our own grief, we feel that we may not be able to do everything we'd like to do for the other person. We may not be able to spend a great deal of quality time with that person, or have frequent long distance calls, or meet his or her needs in the way we wish. Just the same, if we wait to do "a great deal of good at once," we may never do any good at all, because it is quite likely that we'll never make the initial contact. We will always be waiting for a better time, a more opportune period in our own lives. This delay may result in feelings of remorse or embarrassment when later we realize that so much time has gone by that it is going to be nearly impossible to establish a meaningful, caring contact.

 When I am truly concerned about the well-being of another survivor and want to be of help, I will try to reach out in some small way as soon as I can and not worry about making some major move later on. Today I will plan what I'm going to say in my call, or what I will write in my note, or how I will ask another person to relay my message or invitation. Then I will take some action.

He knows what I'm thinking. I know what he's thinking.
We just steer clear of any talk about the death.

Trouble is a part of your life, and if you
don't share it, you don't give the person who
loves you a chance to love you enough.

DINAH SHORE

Some survivors who have lost a child move silently through
their marriage. Some siblings never speak to one another
about the death of a parent. Some friends never bring up the
friend who is missing, and so on. This does not help us heal,
and it does not help those around us to heal. It doesn't give the
person who loves us a chance to show his or her concern, affection, understanding, or helpfulness—and vice versa.

We need to create an opportunity for sharing feelings and
exchanging thoughts. We need to ask for communication. To
make the attempt to communicate and share is far healthier
than moving in the same orbit as one another and never speaking of what disturbs us most or dominates our thoughts.

ও *I will not continue to remain silent. I will give the people who
love me a chance to show me their love, to share my pain and for me
to share theirs. I will ask for what I need. If I don't get it, I will be no
worse off than if I had not asked. I owe it to myself to break the existing tension and to try to close the gap between myself and the
other grieving person. Rather than continuing to fortify our separateness one from the other, I will make it possible to strengthen our
existing bond.*

*His behavior changed after the death. He shut himself off
from everyone.*

People who lead a lonely existence always have something on their
minds that they are eager to talk about.

ANTON CHEKHOV

What do we do about the other survivor whose behavior changes dramatically after the death and who shuts himself or herself off from others whenever possible? This person can be the daughter or son of a dead parent, a sibling, the surviving parent, a close friend or relative, even a business associate.

We need to respect the silence and separateness of others, but we also need to be aware that they may be suffering severely because they feel there is no outlet available to them. They may need to break their silence but not know where to begin. They may have the desire to be among those who are openly mourning the death, but they may not know what to do to join them and they may be unsure whether they are supposed to show their thoughts or feelings. Isolation can have its personal benefits, but not if the isolation is constant and continuous. We can help the lone survivor by recognizing the hazards of retreating into a too-private world. We can be fairly safe in assuming that the other person would benefit from talking about what is on his or her mind. Then we can do whatever is possible to ease and facilitate that process.

It is hard to help someone else when I am grieving myself, but I need to remember for my sake as well as for the sake of the other survivor that we, quite likely, have some thoughts and needs in common. I will reach out and try to make a connection. I will talk about how I feel and invite a response, or I will invite the other person to accompany me to a support group where we can be in a safe and supportive atmosphere. There we will be able to explore further our various grief-related reactions and the current conditions of our daily lives.

It's like there's a competition going on—which one of us misses him most.

Let us not dispute with anyone concerning
the reality of his sufferings; it is with sorrows
as with countries—each man has his own.

CHATEAUBRIAND

Each person has his or her own special burden of grief to carry after a loved one dies. We can compare that burden to a country in which the survivor resides. In that country are all the survivor's very personal memories that involve the loved one. There are regrets, joys, desires, fears, guilts, and perhaps even anger and ambivalence. The climate and terrain of each person's sorrow vary according to that person's experiences, his or her age, the number of previous losses the person has dealt with (or not dealt with), and other stresses at the time of the death, as well as many other factors. We need to respect each person's sorrow and recognize that, as with people of different countries, survivors may speak different languages, value one type of behavior over another, or govern ourselves differently.

And like countries touting their cultures, sometimes one survivor seems to vie with another to see who is the most heartbroken. This permits that survivor to shift away from his or her core feelings. Such behavior focuses the grief outside the survivor and places it alongside the grief of someone else for comparison. We can ignore this behavior if it goes on around us. It is an evasion tactic on the part of the mourner and has nothing to do with us. It will pass.

We must remember that all of us have grief that we live with until our efforts at expression and release, and the passage of time, combine to help us heal.

❧ *I will be respectful of differences in the way others grieve. My grief will not be part of an unspoken "competition" among survivors. While my sorrow is similar to that of those around me, it is uniquely mine. I will deal with my reactions to the death as best I can on my own emotional, psychological, and physical turf.*

I think she's angry at me, and I don't know why.

Anger repressed can poison a relationship
as surely as the cruelest words.

DR. JOYCE BROTHERS

A lot has been said about expressing our anger. But what about the situations after a death in which we sense that another person feels angry at us but never says what is on his or her mind? We feel ignored by a family member. A former friend no longer calls. A co-worker avoids us. A neighbor or roommate treats us differently after the death.

As survivors we have enough emotional pressure. The additional confusion or dismay caused by the changed behavior of someone who once treated us well can add to our burden. When we are feeling the effects of such behavior, we can eliminate the guessing game by opening up a discussion with the other person. We don't have to be accusatory, defensive, or angry. We can merely ask in a reasonable and logical manner for the other person to talk with us about what we are sensing. ("I was wondering if I've done something to offend you.") We can explain our perception of the discord and allow discussion to take place. ("I am feeling as if we don't talk as often as we used to.") We can assure the other person that we value our relationship, or we wouldn't be trying to clarify any problem. ("I miss being with you and talking to you. You're an important person in my life.") We can then work toward the positive resolution of any disagreement.

ॐ *I will not allow a relationship I value to be damaged, to be poisoned. I will take positive steps to open up a discussion and clear up any disagreements.*

It's so discouraging to think I am improving one day and then feel desperate the next day.

If you tell [count] every step, you
will make a long journey of it.
THOMAS FULLER

We've heard it before: grief can only be taken one step at a time. But it is important to add that grief can only be taken one *uncounted* step at a time. Taking an emotional inventory every day can be demoralizing. Being attuned to our own progress is fine, but if we assess ourselves too frequently, we may feel as if we're not making any headway at all. Our various emotional responses and conditions will fluctuate a great deal. It is possible, for example, to go through five or six emotions in an hour for several hours in a day. Imagine how exhausting it would be to try to find a pattern to such confusion and to attempt to gauge our growth.

We need to remind ourselves that we must do what we need to do each day, letting our feelings and responses to the loss of our loved one come as they must. We must not criticize ourselves for seeming to be stuck or for slipping backward. We need to trust that, by experiencing our feelings as they come and letting them happen, we will eventually pass through the roughest times.

∾ *I must not concentrate on the small steps within this journey, but live each day with the knowledge that as long as I feel—and express what I feel in some way—I will come through this difficult time.*

I have a core of strength. I know that now—finally.

The hills are full of marble before
the world blooms with statues.

PHILLIPS BROOKS

With endless days before us and the mammoth task of continuing our way through grief, where, we wonder, will we get the strength? Where will we find the personal resources we so desperately need to get us through this time?

The answer is that the material we need to work with—the core composed of strength, tenacity, will, intellect, and faith— is already there within us. We don't have to hope that it will come along or that we can get it all from a source outside ourselves. We already possess the strong, raw, resilient material we need to work with. Some of it we haven't ever had to use. Some of it we have used so much we think that no part of it can possibly remain, but it is still there.

We need to know, every day, that we can draw upon sources inside ourselves with the assurance that they are there and that they won't run out. We can make it through. We have what we need.

❧ *I have within me all that I need to get through this time of my life. Even though I can benefit tremendously by having others who support me in compassionate, intelligent, and very practical ways, I—all by myself—have the necessary core of belief, courage, and know-how to work myself through my grief. I will agree to use, to my full capacity, my inner resources, never losing faith that they will sustain me. I have made it through challenging times before, and though this time may be the most challenging of all, I can and will do it again.*

*I get a lot of comfort from taking walks and being out
in nature.*

Mountains are giant, restful, absorbent. You can
heave your spirit into a mountain and the mountain
will keep it, folded. . . . mountains are home.

ANNIE DILLARD

*I*t is amazing how calming and restful it can be to go out for
a walk or a drive where there is nothing to see but trees,
mountains, farmland, or the sea. Even if these are not available
where we live, there will still be some restful environment to
which we can retreat. But we may need to put more effort into
locating it.

One woman survivor told of spending an hour visiting the
city aquarium once a week, finding that it calmed her to watch
the movement of the fish, to observe their motion and their
beauty. It gave her relief from daily pressure and time to focus
her thoughts, to gather her strength. A young widower made it
a habit to walk into the large inner courtyard of his office complex on his lunch break and sit by himself on a secluded bench
for a half hour or so. Such an escape, regardless of how small,
can allow precious time for centering our thoughts and emotions and for relieving bodily stress.

When we're at home, it often seems as if it would require
too much effort to go out for a walk; but when we push ourselves, the exercise generates energy rather than dissipating it.
It also helps to lighten our mood and outlook.

◐ *My body is trying to cope with an enormous amount of emotional stress. I need to remember that my body, my mind, and my
spirit are one. I cannot tend to one and neglect another. I will select*

a place that I know has given me pleasure and peace in the past, and I will plan to visit that place at regular intervals whether it be every day, three times a week, or just once a week. Without fail, I will give myself that small gift of serenity without feeling guilt or pressure.

I don't get it; I don't understand life.

What is the meaning of life? . . . The great revelation . . . never did come. Instead there were little daily miracles, illuminations, matches struck unexpectedly in the dark.

VIRGINIA WOOLF

What is life for? Why does death happen to someone who isn't ready for it—who is too young or too valuable in the world or too indispensable to those who love him or her? What is the purpose of suffering, anyway? Why do we have to go through it?

We don't get direct answers to such questions. As we ask them, we know they are impossible. There are no great revelations to be made. But there *are* ways in which we can realize that our lives have meaning, that we are here for a purpose, that we can do good for others—and promote growth and happiness in ourselves.

We don't need to have the answers to the big questions in order to continue meaningful lives, for there is meaning in nearly everything if we are open enough to recognize and appreciate it. We do need to allow ourselves to become alert, to delight in the small rewards and pleasures of life that constitute those daily miracles.

❧ *Despite my not understanding the mysteries of life and death, I can still be illumined by matches struck in the dark. Sometimes I strike them myself; sometimes they are struck by others. Something as simple as provoking a smile in someone who hasn't smiled for a long time is a little miracle of life, a spark of pleasure. I will be open to receiving and creating those kinds of actions. I will see in each of them the answer to the meaning of life. I will understand that they are the lights that will guide me, eventually, beyond my grief.*

I've let things go. I've got a lot to do, but I just can't get started.

Procrastination gives you something to look forward to.

JOAN KONNER

*I*f we're trying to do lots of things in the first year after the death occurs, then we are having unreal expectations for ourselves. We need some time to figure out priorities for our commitments and responsibilities, to think through the best approach to take. When we are grieving, phone calls, errands, shopping, correspondence, domestic chores, and work-related tasks can all pile up into huge mountains that seem insurmountable. But we can make the process easier on ourselves by not looking at the whole mountain at once.

We need to make a list of everything we think we should be doing. Then we can set the goal for ourselves of accomplishing one task a day, or one every three days, or whatever we feel is appropriate for our available time and energy. There is no rule that says we have to be completely efficient. None at all. In fact, aside from the work required on our job, we can be inefficient. We can leave lots of things on our list to do when we get the energy. We can make headway as slowly as we like. With a smile we can tell ourselves (and anyone who pushes us) that procrastination gives us something to look forward to.

~ *I will be realistic about the responsibilities that I have. I will make a deal with myself to do a certain amount a week. I will make the goal as modest as I like. Then I will do my best to stick with my plan, giving myself some kind of break or reward between accomplishments. I can't expect to be as efficient as I was before the death.*

If I don't get something done that I feel needs to be done, I can put it at the top of my list for next week. I can also ask for help if my tasks are too hard or if they bring back memories I would rather not have right now.

We lived the perfect life.

The world of myth is always just behind us. . . . We keep groping
back with our foot for it like first basemen.

C. K. WILLIAMS

*I*n an effort to avoid uncomfortable feelings, we may have
a tendency to turn the life we led with our loved one into
a kind of myth. If we do, we won't recall our lives as whole re-
alities that encompassed a multitude of feelings and conditions. Instead, they will become unreal, invented lives based
on characters whose flaws and fears are invisible.

Myth certainly has its purpose. We can use it to transform
our lives. We can claim to have the life that rises above real life,
that extends its powers outside actual life and transcends the
ordinary in all possible ways. It is pleasant to think of life in
this way. It provides a bright backdrop against which the usually more muted colors of life play out. That is not to say that
our lives do not have their own brightness, their own fantasy,
their mythical qualities; they do. But they also contain the dark
that contrasts sharply with the light.

Our grief is successfully resolved when we acknowledge
the whole range of our lives, when we don't mythologize our
relationships, when we are thankful for the contrasts and differences that made up the rich fabric of our relationship with
our loved one.

ᔗ *As I grieve my loved one, I will mourn the relationship we actually had, the person he or she actually was, the experience we
honestly shared. I will not create a mythology in order to avoid certain aspects of my loss.*

Well, I've been grieving for months, and I don't have any hope for things to get better.

Hope is like the sun, which, as we journey toward it, casts the shadow of our burden behind us.

SAMUEL SMILES

*I*t is nearly impossible to hold out hope on days that are particularly difficult to bear. At such times we feel as if life as we knew it and enjoyed it has been transformed into a seemingly endless period of sadness and despair.

But the more we retreat into the shadow of this belief, the more certain we will become about the impossibility of change. It is important, instead, to prod ourselves forward, to call a friend, to go out of our way to speak to a neighbor, to interact in some way with those around us. We need to reach out and venture out—if only for a short while. For example, we may assign ourselves one small exercise in sociability, such as starting a conversation with someone we haven't talked with for a while. Then we need to carry through by making sure we contact that person before the end of the day.

As we become involved in interacting and communicating with others, we keep ourselves engaged in life—and life itself is hope. It means continuing ahead, leaving behind us the most distressing aspects of today and yesterday. As we move toward life, toward hope, we will find our burden dropping away bit by bit—slowly at first, but then more rapidly until we have whole days in which we are able to experience ourselves inching from the darkness into the light.

❧ *I will not allow myself to withdraw into hopelessness. When I am feeling deep despair, I will make a point of talking to someone else, performing at least one small task, so that I may feel a sense of connection with the people and things around me. I will recognize that I cannot reside permanently in the shadow of sorrow and that as I move toward light, I move toward hope.*

I'm afraid to do things I used to do all the time.

I believe that anyone can conquer fear by doing the things
he fears to do, provided he keeps doing them
until he gets a record of successful experiences behind him.

ELEANOR ROOSEVELT

*A*fter a death we feel less secure, less sure of ourselves. Small actions that used to be so easy can become enormously difficult, especially if they require venturing outside or traveling—taking a plane, subway, or bus, even stepping onto an escalator or entering our own house alone. In our vulnerable state of mind, simply going outside when it is dark can be very frightening.

Those of us who have experienced such fears have learned that it is possible to deal with them successfully, to overcome them so that we can return to our more customary behavior, the behavior we exhibited before the death.

If we feel fear for the first few months after the death, there is no need to force ourselves to do something that we really don't have to do. But after we are further along in the grieving process, we may begin to alleviate our fears by actually engaging in the dreaded activities; for example, entering the house or apartment at night and walking from room to room, proving to ourselves that no harm will come to us. Each time the activity is completed and put behind us, we become stronger. It is true that anything we dread can be robbed of its power by accomplishing it successfully.

❧ *If I fear some activity that has been keeping me from living my life normally since the death and this has gone on for more than a few months, I now need to consider engaging in that activity. By doing so, I will learn that I can accomplish it without suffering any harm or punishment. If I feel unable to do it alone the first couple of times, I will explain my fear to someone I trust and ask that person to accompany me. I will not allow my fear to grow or to dictate a change in my lifestyle.*

How can he be so cold and go on as if nothing has happened?

Believe me, every heart has its secret sorrows,
which the world knows not; and oftentimes we
call a man cold when he is only sad.

HENRY WADSWORTH LONGFELLOW

A thirteen-year-old girl remarked that her father had grown completely cold after her older brother died. "He goes on as if nothing has happened," she raged. "How can he do that? It makes me hate him!"

It's difficult to watch someone who was close to our loved one appear to be unaffected by the death—not speaking about it, not crying, not visiting the grave, or not changing his social behavior. What, we ask ourselves, is wrong with him? Doesn't he have any feelings? Can't he love?

This type of criticism is aimed more often at men than at women, because men in our society often behave as if they're not supposed to have feelings. They are not encouraged to grieve, to share their reactions to loss. After a death, men are usually thrust into (or assume) a position that requires them to oversee the business aspects of the death and to protect the family from outside intrusion. In these two roles, very little time and space and companionship are found for exhibiting feelings.

Any survivor can feel very deeply and not know what to do about it. We should recognize that such a survivor may be grieving invisibly. If efforts to draw the person out in conversation (or get him or her to go to a support group) completely fail, then we can only wait and try again later; but becoming disgusted, disappointed, or angry will be of no help.

∾ *I will remember that all people do not grieve alike. Appearing cold is not the same as feeling nothing. In fact, going on "as if nothing has happened" may be a clue to feeling a great deal and being afraid that such feelings will show. I don't know how another survivor feels, and I need to respect his or her behavior during this grieving period. I will try to encourage the sharing of reactions and concerns, but if that doesn't work, I will be observant for signs, at a later time, which indicate to me that the person wants to communicate.*

I think she's feeling terrible because she's been ignored by our family. I want to help, but maybe that's not what I should do.

He who wishes to secure the good of
others has already secured his own.

CONFUCIUS

𝒲e may feel we need to help someone outside the family who was in some way involved in the death—the driver of the car in which our loved one was a passenger, the live-in companion of our loved one, the babysitter of our child who died. At such a time it is important to remember that showing kindness to another, concern for another, is never wrong. It may be of tremendous help. Less often, in the confusion and hurt that grief causes, our overtures may be rejected.

More likely than not, we can initiate a positive experience. We can show that we are recognizing the other person's grief, that even though we have our own deep feelings of sorrow, we don't wish to deny the needs and feelings of others. Helping another person by some small act of kindness, by volunteering to talk, by inviting the other person over for coffee or a glass of wine can be beneficial to both of us.

ℭ *I will be less hesitant about contacting the other survivor. I will realize that by reaching out to the other person, I am also opening myself up. I am creating an opportunity for both of us to benefit by sharing.*

Most of the time, now, I'm not sure what it is I am supposed to do.

Either I will find a way, or I will make one.
SIR PHILIP SIDNEY

*G*rief has no clear direction. There is no direct path through the many emotional territories that make up our loss. So it is only natural that we would hope for clearer signs, for a road map of sorts that would guide us through the grieving process. But each of us finds our own way or *makes* our own way, depending on our circumstances and our character.

Imagine that as you follow along your path of sorrow, you are pleased because you sense that you are making a bit of headway. Then you round the bend and find that a large tree has fallen across your path. Now you can choose to do one of two things: You can view the tree as an obstacle, and turn around and go in another direction, or you can view the tree as a stepping stone that was delivered into your path. You can step up onto the tree and climb over.

If there is no path at all, if your grief seems to be a solid, impenetrable forest, stand back a moment and remind yourself that a forest is made up of single trees. Each takes up space, it's true, but there is space around each one to allow it to grow, and it is that same space that also allows you to pass. By thinking of the forest as a collection of individual trees, you can slip in among them and cross through to the clearing where sun filters down to the forest floor and brighter days are possible.

❧ *I will think not of what I am "supposed to do," but of what I can do. On days when my way seems blocked, I will not find my way, I will make my way.*

I wanted to say something, but I couldn't.

At all crucial moments in our lives we want
to speak without knowing what to say.

JOYCE CAROL OATES

There are so many times during the grieving period when
we are at a loss for words. We want to say something, we
even *need* to say something, yet we find ourselves unable to figure out exactly what to say. So we say something we wish we
had not said. Or we say nothing at all. We may then make ourselves miserable reliving the incident in which we said the
wrong thing, or didn't say enough, or said too much. It could
have happened in a tense family situation, with a well-meaning
visitor, or even with some social acquaintance who we feel in-
truded upon our privacy or our thoughts.

As we look back over the incident, we need to accept that
it was another one of those inevitable outcomes of being
human. None of us can say exactly what we feel—or what
needs to be said—all of the time. Unfortunately, the more critical the moment, the less likely we are to be able to think of the
appropriate words. So all we can do is realize that each of us
has this problem and accept that we did the best we could at
the time and with the personal resources we had available. If
we responded in a way that we now believe was wrong or inappropriate, and we strongly feel that we need to correct it, we
can send a note to clarify what we meant, or apologize, or do
whatever seems necessary to improve the situation.

*I will not feel remorse because I didn't say the "right thing" at
a certain time. If need be, I will make some gesture to rectify it. But
I should recognize that anything I do or say during the grieving pe-*

riod is done and said at a time when I have very limited energy, willpower, clarity of thought, or patience with conversation. If I don't live up to my own expectations, I will at least recognize that others will judge me less harshly than I judge myself.

It's so overwhelming, trying to clear out his room.

I never gave away anything without wishing I had kept it;
nor kept it without wishing I had given it away.

LOUISE BROOKS

We are left after a death with a lot to sort through. Some of the sorting involves material things such as physical belongings. We have to go through closets or drawers, or we need to collect our loved one's possessions from some other place or person. Such tasks are extremely debilitating. They can be so overwhelming that they paralyze our actions, so that many of us put off disposing of things for as long as we can.

There is also another kind of sorting that goes on. This sorting is mental and emotional. We decide what to keep and what to give away. We may also examine some of what we've kept—resentment or guilt, for example—and we know it's time to let it go.

We move through these various sorting processes, giving attention to each item, investing our energy in tasks that seem enormous, lonely, and thankless, but that must eventually be done.

It is necessary for us to be kind to ourselves in the process by taking frequent breaks and inviting someone to keep us company during or after the hardest part of our sorting.

❧ *I will do both the material and mental sorting piece by piece, without putting pressure on myself to do it perfectly. As I examine each item or thought or deed, I will be kind to myself. The choices I have made, am making, and will continue to make represent my best efforts.*

I came to know my mother by the things she left behind.

After [her] death I began to see her as she had really been. . . .
It was less like losing someone than discovering someone.
NANCY HALE

*I*n the midst of mourning there can also be the process of discovery. As we go through the possessions of our loved ones or review their lives in other ways, we may discover facets we didn't know existed. We may become aware, for the first time, of certain people, events, or things in our loved one's life that had particular significance. Without anticipating it, we may uncover answers to puzzling questions we always had about our loved one.

This process of discovery can be either positive or negative. It can permit joy or induce sorrow. On the one hand, it gives us a clearer picture of our loved one; it affords us an open, honest look at a whole person who may have been a very complex mix of actions, opinions, possessions, and relationships.

On the other hand, the process of discovery does not always have to be quite that bold. It may not be implemented by the uncovering of anything tangible. It can simply be that in our reflections on our loved one we reach certain realizations, have new awarenesses, and get a different perspective. Or we can find ourselves at a level of maturity that allows us to see our loved one in a new light.

I will allow myself to acknowledge my discoveries about my loved one's traits, character, likes, dislikes, preoccupations, loves, and concerns. Even though the new information may be in conflict with my previous beliefs and perceptions, I can reflect on the fuller, more complete picture that I now have.

I wish I had known then what I know now about the reason he did certain things.

Life can only be understood backwards,
but it must be lived forwards.

SØREN KIERKEGAARD

*R*etrospection is helpful for fitting ourselves and our life experience into the larger picture. We cannot hope to understand our lives as thoroughly at the moment of everyday involvement. When we are close to another person but our time is consumed by daily activities, our schedules full and our energies taxed, we may have the greatest intentions in the world to get beyond the surface of some things, to investigate the other person's feelings, to discuss motivations and behavioral patterns, but we don't have the opportunity to do so.

This is true sometimes even within a marriage, or between siblings or close friends: we presume to understand from our observation their casual speech, their surface expressions, their standard activities. But retrospection condenses the years of the relationship. It may supply us with a context for deeper understanding of the ways the loved one thought and acted. And with this greater comprehension often comes remorse, regret for not having been closer in tune when the loved one was alive.

We can discuss our reservations or remorse and get them out in the open, but focusing on them exclusively only prevents us from living in the present and looking forward to the future. We may have new information now that makes it possible for us to put together a picture of the relationship we had with our loved one that differed from the one we thought we had. It isn't necessarily better or worse—it is just different. And we can forgive ourselves for not knowing then what we know now.

෴ *I must simply live my life as best I can on a daily basis without punishing myself for failing to understand something when it occurred in the past. If I had a thorough understanding of everything in my past at the time it happened, I would not have regrets; but I would also not have rewards, for there would have been no exploration or risk taking necessary.*

The way I feel about life has changed forever. It means so much more to me now.

There is no cure for birth and death save to enjoy the interval.
The dark background which death supplies
brings out the tender colours of life in all their purity.

GEORGE SANTAYANA

*N*othing changes our view of life more than surviving the death of a loved one or having a close brush with death ourselves. One young mother remarked that even the colors of the things in her environment appeared to be more brilliant after she came close to dying.

As survivors, we may have similar experiences. We may find ourselves in awe of people or things we've never focused on before. As we "reenter the world" after suffering a loss, we will encounter people and activities and judge them differently. We will be likely to have a reverence for aspects of our existence previously taken for granted.

☙ *I will recognize that I have been changed by death, that many of my perceptions and values are changed. I will take time to appreciate the "tender colours of life," finding solace in their beauty and strength in their presence.*

How do you know you're healed?

What wound did ever heal but by degrees.

WILLIAM SHAKESPEARE

When we hurt ourselves physically, when we scrape or scratch ourselves, we don't expect to look at the abrasion two minutes later and find that it has healed. If we have major surgery, we don't expect to be wholly recovered within weeks. Similarly, when we have a surgery of the heart and soul, when we lose a loved one, we cannot expect to heal quickly.

But just as the body does repair itself, just as new cells replace damaged cells and skin heals over and we regain the use of our physical selves, so it is with grief. Bit by bit we are being repaired. It may happen so slowly at first we may not recognize it or see evidence of it, but it will happen.

༅ *I must trust the process of grief and know that, even though I may not think or feel that I am making any progress, healing is taking place within me. That healing is by degrees, and most of the time it is invisible, but as I review and express my reactions to death, I am being repaired. My heart and my mind are becoming accustomed to my loss, and I am learning to use my special resources to continue life in a changed way.*

I haven't done anything worthwhile since he died,
so what's the use?

Each small task of everyday life is part
of the total harmony of the universe.
SAINT TÉRÈSE OF LISIEUX

*S*ometimes it's easy to convince ourselves that our existence
is completely and totally unimportant, that because we're
not making some remarkable contribution our lives are meaningless. Survivors often remark: "Nothing makes any difference. I can't change anything. There's no use knocking yourself
out."

We've all had these sentiments or heard others assert them.
But each of us does make a difference. The universe is only
made up of its parts, and each of us is one of those parts. Each
small task we perform is a fragment of the whole, a part of
everything around us.

Imagine looking down at the world from an aerial view
and watching all the trillions and trillions of actions being
performed during any split second. Next, imagine that each person performing a task suddenly said to himself or herself, "I'm
not doing anything worthwhile, so what's the use?" As a result,
all of the activity in progress is suddenly halted for as far as
your eye can see. The hum and order, the preparation and creation are stopped everywhere. Now nothing is in a state of pro-
duction or change, growth or birth, or even death. Nothing
happens. And all of us find ourselves occupying a void in

which the harmony of people's actions is no longer necessary or even possible.

❧ *What I do is important, however insignificant I think it is. Each small task has its place in the overall order of things. I might argue that I could stop everything I do every day and no one would notice. The world would not come to an end. But my contribution, through my actions, is part of living in an active world. It is part of having a conscience and a future. What I do is worthwhile because it contributes to the life processes of those around me.*

I keep thinking about things I wish I could say to her.
The same thoughts keep coming up over and over.

Write down the thoughts of the moment.
Those that come unsought for are commonly the most valuable.
FRANCIS BACON

S ometimes there is some particular information we grapple with or emotion we fasten on, and we want desperately to be able to talk it over with our lost loved one.

A thought that keeps recurring or a dream that keeps repeating deserves our attention and time. When we have thoughts that persist in coming or the same dream themes reappear week after week, we need to acknowledge them and give them room to express themselves.

We can write them down. As we do, we'll find that our thoughts will take a new turn. We will be able to examine what we have written, to add to it, to take it apart, to understand it. And, equally important, the thought or dream will lose its power to dominate our minds. We will have control over it as we read it and work with it.

❧ *When I have a thought or a dream that keeps coming up again and again, I will give it room. I will write it down and read it to myself, share it within a supportive environment, or explore it privately. Once I have brought it out into the open, it will have lost its power to repeatedly overshadow my other thoughts or consume my mental energy.*

Is there any way to get rid of these feelings of guilt?
I've been guilty for a year now.

You have not lived a perfect day . . . unless
you have done something for someone who
will never be able to repay you.

RUTH SMELTZER

We may be suffering greatly from feelings of remorse about being neglectful, cold, or unavailable to our loved one. Regardless of whether these feelings are imaginary or real, they are causing us deep pain. We have done something—or we *think* we have done something—that we cannot undo. As a result, we feel continually tormented.

To live with such persistent feelings is a daily trial. We accuse ourselves and cannot, it seems, redeem ourselves. But there is a way out: we can focus outside ourselves on another person or group in need of some kind of physical, emotional, or social assistance. We can take a look at that person or group of people to see what we can offer. We can see in what way we can do for another life (or lives) that which we think we have failed to do in the past. By trying to do something for someone who is not in a position to repay us, we are giving ourselves the chance to redeem our mistakes and compensate for our flaws. We are giving ourselves the chance to increase our own self-esteem so that we can be proud of ourselves rather than ashamed.

∾ *I have done things in the past that I wish I could undo—but it is too late. I can, however, do new things in my life that help me to reverse the image I have of myself. I can identify someone or some* group of people who can use my capabilities, talents, or compassion. Then I can dedicate my time, energy, and attention to the needs of those others. I will not contribute money; I will give of myself. I will experience, firsthand, the benefits of giving, the pure pleasure that comes from increasing the quality of someone else's life.

Nothing will ever change. This is the way it is.

Human misery must somewhere have a stop:
There is no wind that always blows a storm.

EURIPIDES

*I*t is almost impossible, sometimes, to imagine that our situation can change. But it does, finally. After a stormy period of mixed feelings or prolonged sadness, there comes a calm. After we become convinced that we are at the very brink of eternal despair, or fear, or guilt, or sadness, we are given a reprieve. We have a breathing space that eventually leads to whole days that have personal value and offer us the opportunity for affection. Then we recognize that no period of misery is endless and unrelenting; it is, instead, changeable.

As surely as we have been made to despair in the past, we can be uplifted.

∾ *When I think I can stand no more, I will sit quietly and comfortably in a room by myself. I will close my eyes and concentrate on relaxing my body. I will remind myself that a time of relief will follow the long periods of despair. Every day I have experienced emotional pain will be replaced by a day that offers me relief, solace, and inspiration. I need to have faith that I will have hours, days, and eventually months of inner peace.*

How am I supposed to ever act happy again?

Happiness is not a state to arrive at,
but a manner of traveling.

MARGARET LEE RUNBECK

*I*t is difficult to listen to people telling us we will feel better. Such advice is especially hard to hear when we can't imagine how in the world we could ever smile with any conviction or laugh without guilt.

But as we emerge from the grieving process and begin to reinvest in our own future again, to have hopes and dreams and plans, to talk with friends and look forward to events, it's important to remember that happiness isn't solely a property of memory. That is, our happiness is more than that which we remember; it is our way of being, our dedication to ourselves. As we go through each day ahead, we need not try to reach happiness as a destination, but rather live it as a journey.

ᘓ *I will remember that my happiness is not a thing but a process. It is the way in which I travel through the days ahead. Some of the travels will be easier, lighter, and more rewarding than others, but each day the journey is my own and I am its guide.*

It's hard to get interested in people again, to trust them.

I believe in people, which I suppose
is a way of believing in God.

VERA RANDAL

*A*fter having survived the trials that grief puts us through,
it is hard for us to envision a whole life again that presents itself as an opportunity, that opens up doors to new possibilities and in which people play an important part. Sometimes
it's hard to trust other people, events, and forces greater than
ourselves, to trust that we will be able to conduct our lives
again with confidence and that tragedy will not return to
strike us.

But we need now to receive people into our lives and look
forward to spending time with them. We need to reacquaint
ourselves with those whose friendships, business relationships,
and community involvements sustain our lives. Humans are,
by nature, sociable creatures. We should not try to deny that
instinct.

❧ *I have been through a time that has tested my endurance,
courage, and beliefs; but now it is time to renew my faith in others
and in the community that surrounds me. I will recognize that returning to a full life involves belief and trust in other people as well
as myself.*

I never thought I'd ever have to settle for this.

One doesn't discover new lands without consenting
to lose sight of the shore for a very long time.
ANDRÉ GIDE

While grieving, we feel adrift, unsure of our direction. We may even be uncertain about our survival. To be in such a state is terrifying. Yet, in better days, we recognize that the feelings of uncertainty are a part of the necessary transition from life as we knew it to life as it will now be.

With this casting about, we lose sight of the shore we were used to, the familiar life we led before our loss. But losing sight of that shore is the first step toward discovering the new ways we will live—not survive, but live. There are comfortable zones of love, pleasure, and independence in which we will be able to live our lives and eventually to flourish. It is hard to imagine such a possibility soon after a loss, but as each month goes by and we cast about for our new directions, we can get a clearer vision of the ways we can ground ourselves in new and promising territory.

❧ *By clinging to what is behind me, I make it impossible to seek a stable place from which to begin anew. I will consent to lose sight of the familiar shore so that I may arrive safely and surely at my new, changed choice of destinations.*

When I wake up knowing that this will be a better day,
it helps to make it a better day.

Believe that life is worth living,
and your belief will help create the fact.

WILLIAM JAMES

When we are grieving, we—out of self-protection—create our own reality. At first, we do it to get through the turmoil, to survive; later, we do it differently as we explore our grief and try to figure out the new ways in which we will need to live our life.

Similarly, as we work toward the resolution of loss, we can create the reality that will serve as the bedrock of our changed life. We can do this by beginning each day with the belief in the value of our life and with trust in our own behavior. We can do it with the assurance that there will be pleasure and promise, love and reward. By thinking it is so, we will make it possible. We will make it fact.

❧ *I will not fear life. Instead I will recognize all the many ways in which my life is worth living. I will enter into each new day with the belief that my life holds opportunities, pleasures, enjoyable challenges, and rewarding moments. With the convictions of my belief, I can begin to shape my days to fit my desires and my needs.*

THREE

Resolving

Without any warning, I began to cry.

The ocean has its ebbings—so has grief.
PROVERB

We may go along in a stable emotional state for several months or even a year or so, and then suddenly something we see or hear or smell—some situation or location—will remind us of our loved one and we'll find ourselves in tears.

One widow tells of starting to cry in the supermarket, another in the bank, another in the post office. A father tells of breaking down at a baseball stadium, another father at a friend's wedding. A grieving sister tells of having to pull over while driving on the freeway because of emotion triggered by a song that came on the radio. There is no preparation for these sudden bursts of sadness, these spontaneous crying sessions. They are simply evidence that the pain of our loss can still be tapped by external events. Even though our grief may be out of our consciousness most of the time, it is still with us to some degree.

But just as these floods of sadness rush forward, they also ebb away. They occur with less and less frequency, allowing us to return to more normal functioning with a reduced threat of "sadness attacks." When we are in the midst of a raw emotional episode, we need to remember that the surge of sadness will wash backward just as it surged forward. We will, once again, be able to regain our composure and trust ourselves to become fully engaged in the moment.

∽ *When I experience a flood of unexpected sadness, I will not become afraid or disappointed. I will be assured that it will pass, and eventually the unpredictable surges will lessen. The ocean of my grief will recede, leaving me cleansed of sadness. When I experience recurrences, it is not because I have not healed; it is because I have an unlimited reserve of devotion that will always be there for my loved one who died. It is evidence of the bond we shared.*

Sometimes my loneliness cuts so deep at night I think I can't make it through.

Man's loneliness is but his fear of life.
EUGENE O'NEILL

At first glance, O'Neill's statement seems almost to be mean-spirited, bordering on accusation. It sounds as if lonely humans are being accused of cowardice.

But, in many respects, loneliness *is* a fear of life, our changed life in particular. Once we see how the two are linked, we can recognize the ways in which we can help ourselves. We can give ourselves the chance for small successes during the day—getting through challenging moments, wresting control of difficult situations, gaining a foothold in progress toward even the most minor goal.

Even though we are lonely for our loved one and for the life we both shared, we can recognize that the changed life may be frightening in many ways. We need to exercise control over the small challenges in our lives in order to gain a sense of power in coping with those that are much larger.

❧ *Gradually, I will be able to face, without fear, bigger and bigger segments of my life. I will give myself permission to make changes slowly and deliberately until I can rid myself of the fear that is so broad and deep that it intensifies my loneliness. By taking charge of the small situations, I can gain confidence in dealing with the larger ones.*

I think about how short life is.

Thus we live, for ever taking leave.
RAINER MARIA RILKE

*O*ur mortality has been made more evident by our loved one's dying. In fact, all lives appear less permanent now. We may find ourselves standing back from the small microcosm of our world and seeing the larger universe of our lives. We look backward at the generations before us and into the future at the generations that will follow us. Each birth, each major life event takes on new meaning.

⌘ *The perspective of my life has been enlarged. The brevity of all lives has been underscored. I will use what I have learned to enhance the quality of my life as well as the effect it may have on those in the next generation.*

I'm better. I don't hurt as much, but I can never really be happy again.

Happiness is not having what you
want, but wanting what you have.

HYMAN JUDAH SCHACHTEL

We have grieved our loss and are now trying to return to our daily lives with our selves intact and functioning, but we look at what lies ahead for us and think we can never really be happy. We can't, we think, experience true personal happiness because all that would make us happy is gone. More than anything, happiness is having our loved one alive and with us. It's leading our lives the way they once were.

That is the ultimate happiness, but there are other visions of happiness as well. We can look at what we have been given in the relationship with our loved one and, most important, at what we brought away to use permanently in our lives. We can allow ourselves to want what we now have.

❧ *I will realize that I may need to relearn my own happiness. I can assess what I have salvaged from the devastation of loss and what I value most that is still with me. I will recognize that happiness is truly appreciating and desiring what I now have, the positive legacy of my relationship.*

I'm so afraid we will forget her, that someday we won't be able to remember all that we want to remember. I feel her memory slipping from us.

He who has gone, so we but cherish his
memory, abides with us, more potent,
nay, more present, than the living man.

We may fear we will forget something that we want desperately to remember about our loved one. We are afraid we will not be able to recall a certain look, or habit, or action—something the person said, the way it was said. Yet, when we try to hold on to pieces of our memory too tightly, we squeeze them away.

It is better for us to help our memories live. We can do this by recording on tape, or in writing, the things our loved one said, the way he or she looked or acted. We may record our special moments, the times we most enjoyed together. We may assemble notes, photographs, letters, and clippings in one central place so that we will have a tangible memory bank that we can visit any time we wish. We can also invite others who knew our loved one to contribute their special memories and observations.

❧ *When I am afraid that I will forget something of my loved one—a word, a moment, a look, a habit, a gesture—I will record it. In this way, I will build a living treasure that will provide comfort to me and to others in the days and years ahead.*

I want to write about her, but I don't know where to begin.

Praise day at night, and life at the end.

PROVERB

WW riting about our loved ones can be tremendously helpful in reliving events, relieving anxiety, and focusing our thoughts. We may wish to write about our loved one so that others may become acquainted with him or her. Or we may wish to write only for our own benefit and not show our writing to anyone.

We may begin by mentally reviewing the various facets of our loved one's character, personality, and life—including childhood, schooling, interests, unique capabilities and habits, family relationships, loving relationships, work, and so on, depending on the extent to which we were familiar with his or her entire life.

We may decide to use portions of our writing as a way of memorializing our loved one and honoring his or her life. If so, we can compose a letter, booklet, or poem that we can duplicate and give out to those who were closest to our loved one. Such an undertaking may be both enlightening and inspirational to those with whom we share it.

❧ *As I review my loved one's life, I will write down all the helpful, thoughtful, loving, and generous aspects of his or her character and actions. I will think of my writing as a song of praise, a gift to my loved one for having been in the world and for having affected the lives of others in a variety of ways. I may choose to share what I have written with others or to keep it to myself.*

I have lost a part of myself.

All changes . . . have their melancholy, for what
we leave behind us is a part of ourselves; we must
die to one life before we can enter another.

ANATOLE FRANCE

We lose a part of ourselves when our loved one dies. Now we must make our way from the life we were familiar with to the life that forms a question mark. And we cannot fully enter our changed life and go forward into it until we have let go of the previous life with our loved one.

Letting go does not mean no longer loving. It does not mean that we don't recall and care and yearn and cry. It means that we acknowledge that our life now has another added dimension. Incorporated into our present life are the most wonderful parts of the life we lived when our loved one was with us on earth. We can go forward only by acknowledging that we are not simply leaving behind a part of ourselves, we are carrying into the future a new part of ourselves that represents the bond we shared with our loved one. We let go of one segment of our life to create and perpetuate another.

❧ *It is necessary for me to give up and let go of life as I lived it with my loved one. Even though I wish it were not so, that life has been lived out. I now carry forward with me all that was wonderful, positive, loving, and strong from that relationship. I take it with me everywhere I go. I enter into my changed life, bringing all the most laudable, hopeful, good, and rewarding parts of the past into the future.*

One day, about a year after the death, I realized I was feeding my own misery. I knew I needed to think about helping someone else and to quit focusing so much on myself.

It is one of the beautiful compensations of
this life that no one can sincerely try to
help another without helping himself.

CHARLES DUDLEY WARNER

$\mathcal{J}$t is a natural occurrence during grief, a time when we have extremely limited energy, to feel that we have no power to change anything or to accomplish anything worthwhile. So, we think, why try?

It does no harm for us to feel this way for a short interval, but when the same inertia continues for a long period, we need to make a concentrated effort to work our way out of the pit of despair. We can do this by assessing what needs to be done to help others around us. We can ask ourselves who else is hurting because of this death? Who else is having a difficult time emotionally, for some reason other than this death? Which person among my friends, family, neighbors, or co-workers is in particular need right now of a kind act?

❧ *When I am feeling down and can't seem to pull myself up, I will look around me to see whom I can reach out to help. There are others who are hurting after this death. And there are people in my life who are currently going through other difficult times. I will make a conscious effort to help another person feel better by taking some action purely for the other person's benefit. I know that as I assist another, I am also assisting myself.*

Sometimes now, nearly two years later, I look back and wish we would have had the chance to . . .

Nostalgia . . . seems usually to be an expression
of regret for opportunities missed, rather than
regret for past accomplishments or pleasures.

ANTHONY STORR

When we have lived through the very worst of our grief and we pause to look back over the life we shared with our loved one, we may still find ourselves feeling regretful for something the two of us did not have the chance to do together—for not making a move that would have been desirable, for missing the opportunity we would have shared as a result of a different job decision, for not taking vacations together, for not experiencing parenthood, for not attending our loved one's sports events or concerts, or for not taking a more active part in our sibling's life. This is the type of painful reflection that most mourners engage in from time to time.

Possessing a certain degree of regret is understandable, but why don't we make the choice to look back with the same intensity on successes, worthwhile encounters, or particularly pleasurable moments? Why not balance them against the opportunities missed? Why not recognize that no one's life can be all one way or another? No life is all opportunities missed, just as no life is all accomplishments and pleasures.

❧ *When I slide into nostalgia and begin to regret some part of life I feel was bypassed because of my own—or my loved one's—ineptitude or distraction, I will remind myself to recall the accomplishments and pleasures. I will remember each detail of them over and over again, until any feelings of remorse are counterbalanced by worthwhile recollections.*

I talk to him and I talk about him. I still say "we"
instead of "I."

I must warn you not to be surprised if I
speak about the Dead as if they were alive.

V. S. YANOVSKY

*E*ven after we've worked our way through our jumble of
grief-related reactions and feelings and we believe we've
finally assimilated the fact of our loved one's death into our
present lives, we still have flashes of thinking about our loved
ones as if they were still alive.

We may make a mental note of something we want to tell
them when we see them, when they telephone, or when they
come around the corner or up the stairs. We may find ourselves talking to them in our heads or even aloud. When we
speak of them to others, we forget and use the present or future tense, saying, he thinks, she is, or we will.

Such slips are normal and natural. They reflect the interde-
pendency we shared with our loved one and the depth of our
bond. As time goes by, these harmless lapses will become less
frequent.

❧ *I accept that it may take me quite a while to assimilate my
loved one's death fully, or to remember to speak in the past tense
about my loved one because he or she is forever present in my heart.
If others are worried about me when I do it, I can just tell them not
to be concerned or surprised and to "give me time." By speaking in
the present tense, I am keeping my loved one as my companion a bit
longer, and it does not harm me or anyone else. Eventually, I will no
longer have the need to do it.*

It's taken me a very long time to appreciate what we had together instead of regretting what we couldn't have any longer.

What a wonderful life I've had!
I only wish I'd realized it sooner.

COLETTE

*I*t takes a long time to come to terms with our new status after a death. Only gradually are we able to reach an emotional plateau where we can stop and examine that which has gone before—a stage that lets us evaluate our relationship with our loved one. We identify the strongest parts of our relationship, the most pleasant parts, and the various ways in which we expressed love.

When we do that, we are taking a kind of inventory of our emotional harvest. What have we gathered? Where did we gather it? What have we stored to keep us through the more difficult times? These are all valuable questions. They help us to see the biggest possible picture of our lives, the one that includes not just this time that has been difficult, but a whole range of experiences that have involved a wide variety of people, places, things, ideas, rewards, and pleasures.

❧ *Now that I have the worst part of my grief behind me, I will see my life as a whole, allow myself to feel and express happiness without feeling inhibited or guilty. My life has brought many lessons and trials, but it has also brought many gifts. I will acknowledge those gifts now one by one.*

*Now that she's gone, I don't think I could ever love that
way again.*

The joy that is dead weighs heavy, and bids fair
to crush us, if we cause it to be with us forever.

MAURICE MAETERLINCK

The kind of love and pleasure we had with our loved one cannot be duplicated, regardless of how many people we meet, how many brothers and sisters we feel close to, how many children we have, how many times we fall in love, and so on. But that does not mean our lives are destined to be without joy.

As we come out on the other side of our grief—and we *will* come out on the other side—we are certain, once again, to find pleasure in small things. We will be able to be enthusiastic about something we are doing or something someone else is doing. We will be able to generate excitement with our own thoughts and ideas. And eventually, we will open up more and more to those around us who will play an active part in our future and who themselves will be the source of new love and new joy.

∾ *The mere fact that I have grieved so deeply over the loss of my loved one proves that I am capable of powerful feeling. I will not give up on that part of myself that is so valuable. I will not close it off or pretend that it is not there. I still have the capacity to experience pleasure and to love. Even though I will not have the same life I had with my loved one, I will have a life that continually opens itself to possibility.*

I never thought grief could teach me so much.

It is good to grow wise by sorrow.

AESCHYLUS

*A*t the beginning of our grieving process, we think only about getting through it, surviving the loss of our loved one, and coming out of the experience in one piece without giving up or going crazy. We don't think grief can teach us anything. We don't know or care that it will be a silent educator. That is the last thing on our minds. But then it happens.

One of the most crucial things we learn is that we have resources within ourselves that we didn't know existed. These resources, once tapped, serve us well throughout the rest of our lives.

We survivors also develop a unique wisdom that comes only as a result of loss. We recognize this in one another as we talk in support groups, meet randomly in social situations, or work side by side. We find it difficult to define this "survivors' wisdom" except to say that it has to do with valuing the very essence of life, of having a clearer understanding of life's purpose. And once gained, this is a knowledge no survivor would wish to discard even if it were possible to do so.

∾ *Going through this loss is one of the most difficult things I will ever do. It is one of the most instructive. I have learned lessons about myself and the way I think and act that have been invaluable. I have discovered that I have strength and patience and perseverance. I know that I possess a source of wisdom that will be with me for the rest of my life and upon which I can draw whenever I wish.*

Death has made me realize how important choice is.

The strongest principle of growth lies in human choice.
GEORGE ELIOT

*D*eath shines a light on the flaws of our life. This is true for all of us. We recognize those parts of our lives—sometimes years and years—that we now think were not spent the way they should have been spent. Or we take a look at some of our ways of thinking or acting that had always seemed so important, and they no longer have any importance to us at all.

Death provides for us the opportunity to effect a transformation, to change those aspects of our existence that we are not pleased with. After enduring the death of our loved one, working through the loss and coming out on the other side, we see the choices we made along the way. We can now select the choices we wish to make in the future. We can design our lives with new strength and assurance and more pride in ourselves.

❧ *This is a time for choice. It is a time for me to examine those things that I wish to change and to choose ways in which they will be changed. I will make choices that enrich my life, give me added strength, validate my worthiness, and permit me to look forward to the future.*

I'm a much different person with different values, a better person.

Crises refine life. In them you discover what you are.
ALLAN KNIGHT CHALMERS

Nothing clarifies our values more quickly than death. As we survive the loss of our loved one, we rethink the way we've planned our life. We may reexamine our goals or our methods for attaining our goals. And we may discover a new self inside our former self, because making our way through this crisis can change us internally. We may have more solid views, better-defined goals, stronger opinions, fresh approaches, and new boundaries for behavior. As survivors, our masks are removed, our social veneer is worn thin, and our willingness to "fit in" may be replaced with a solid individualism. This is what I am. This is who I am. This is what I know is right for me. Why? Because I have endured the loss of my loved one, and that has sharpened my view of the world and my place in it.

❧ *As I keep delving into myself, going deeper into what I think and feel, I emerge with the knowledge of what I need and want. I acknowledge my discoveries and accept my new desires. Most of all, I allow myself to assess and enjoy the positive ways in which I have changed.*

How can I make others understand the pleasure I get from certain things?

No facts, however indubitably detected, no effort
of reason, however magnificently maintained,
can prove that Bach's music is beautiful.

EDITH WHARTON

A man who lost his wife and then went through a long and very difficult grieving process remarked how music "saved his soul." He explained that through all the days of his grieving, music had been his constant companion. For many hours, he sat and listened. He went to bed with music; he woke up with it. It became an indispensable, enriching part of his life, which it had not been previously.

We need to incorporate into our lives those things that provoke similar responses. We don't have to be able to explain to someone else what we're doing or prove its value. The only requirement is that we allow ourselves to find pleasure and sustenance in the activity, as did the widower with his music. One woman who was grieving the loss of her sister found it soothing to work with various kinds of fabrics, to run her fingers over them, to arrange them into pleasing designs for quilts. Another woman who had lost both parents had a compelling need to be by the sea, just to stand and look at it, or to walk at the water's edge, poking at rocks and shells. Other survivors have immersed themselves in other ways—taking a sudden interest in studying the stars (as if to find out "what's out there"), watching trains, or gaining solace from camping out on the desert. Whatever it is that pleases or soothes us should be integrated into our lives. It doesn't have to cost anything. And we don't have to be able to prove to others around us that something is beautiful, calming, or nourishing. The proof is in how it makes us feel. We must give it to ourselves.

    ∾ *Today I will devote some time to bringing into my life that which gives me solace, which soothes and nourishes me. I will give myself the freedom to become completely immersed in the activity if I wish. I can share it with someone else if I choose to, but I don't need to. What I choose to do in this regard, I do simply because it suits me. It doesn't have to be valued by others. I don't need to prove beauty or serenity in order to enjoy it. I only need to make it a part of my life.*

I no longer feel the need to have all the big questions answered.

I used to trouble about what life was for—
now being alive seems sufficient reason.
JOANNA FIELD

A father who lost both children in an accident spent months and months trying to figure out why he was still here, what he had done to deserve punishment, what his life was for, what anyone's life was for. Then, finally, he reached the point where he no longer felt the need to have all his questions answered. He was able to fit himself into a life pattern and, difficult though it was, to propel himself into the days ahead of him. It wasn't resignation that he experienced, but the realization that he had been given life and he didn't need to question its purpose—only to live it to its fullest potential.

When we return to a fairly normal routine involving customary people, places, and things, we will most likely find ourselves being more indulgent about our own purposes. We may be less structured in our thinking, and more creative.

By living through our grief, we learn the value of life for its own sake—without grand purposes or unrealistic expectations. On those days when we are emerging from the reclusiveness that death engenders, we can be content with simply being alive.

❧ *I won't torment myself with major philosophical questions. I will simply be in life in a way that I've never been in it before. I will look at each day as a new gift.*

I feel he is around me, with me, maybe even protecting me.

He had ceased to meet us in particular places
in order to meet us everywhere.

C. S. LEWIS

*A*t first, one of the questions we may ask—silently or aloud—is this: Where did my loved one go? Where is he or she now? It becomes tremendously important to try to determine and then to accept where our loved one went after he or she died. What is the location, we wonder, of all those who die? And how do we know?

But eventually, a different understanding arises and matures regarding our loved one's existence. We realize that our loved one may not be here sitting in a chair or coming through the door or walking down the street, but he or she is here just the same. The spirit of the person whose life we intimately shared never dissolves, never departs, never deserts us. The person may not be here in front of us any longer, because he or she is everywhere.

∾ *I will not question the location of my loved one; instead, I'll accept the presence of my loved one all around me in everything I do, everywhere I go, as a companion whom I do not need to admit into my house or heart, because he or she is already there.*

Even with the pain, I would not have traded this time of sorrow.

A youth was questioning a lonely old man.
"What is life's heaviest burden?" he asked.
And the old fellow answered sadly, "To have nothing to carry."

ANONYMOUS

*E*ven though our grief is a burden and an extremely heavy one that we have been carrying now for some time, it doesn't hurt for us to stop occasionally, shift the weight of our load, and reflect for a moment about what all of this means.

Once again, we can remind ourselves that our grief, as horrendous as it has been and still may be, represents a valuable dimension in our lives. It is a dimension that would not have been there if we had not had the opportunity to love as we did. So our grief is a burden we continue to carry with gratitude. If we had not known our loved one, if we had never had the opportunity in our lives for the emotion and attachment to create this burden, how very desolate our lives would have been. William Faulkner underscored this truth when he said, "Between grief and nothing I will take grief."

❧ *The love I shared was a gift. I have a heavy load to bear now, but I will carry it reminding myself, whenever I need to, that the alternative would be living in this world without having had this particular loving relationship. The emotional pain I have lived through and am now still facing from time to time represents the love that was and is the richest portion of my life.*

Sometimes I go away for two or three days so I can just sit and think and write without having to worry about anyone other than myself.

Thinking is the talking of the soul with itself.
PLATO

For some of us, the period during which we resolve our loss provides us with an opportunity for self-understanding, for the further development of our compassion and of a capacity to create a stronger link with those around us. In that sense it is a rich period that takes us down to the very depths of our being and prompts us to look into every dark corner of our souls—to look toward the discoveries we have made.

The death of our loved one may provoke extensive, complicated self-explorations. By writing out our thoughts, we can gain a wonderful sense of release. Such writings may include situations we pose for ourselves. Or they may be letters to ourselves that incorporate observations, perceptions, and identification of our strengths and weaknesses.

୰ *When I wish to retreat into myself for the purposes of self-exploration, I will arrange a time and place for myself that allows for that. I can explore my thoughts extensively in a journal. Among other benefits, this exercise will help me to gain new insights and affirm certain beliefs.*

I used to dread the future.

The best thing about the future is
that it only comes one day at a time.

ABRAHAM LINCOLN

Through our grief we often see the days that are ahead of us as something to dread, a solid block of future that we are going to have to "get through" some way or another. But our future is not in a solid block. It is not all in one chunk that we must push before us like weary work animals doing our grim duty. The future is a series of opportunities that come one day at a time.

One woman survivor said, "I found the best way to brighten my outlook about living was to do this: First I made a conscious effort to do something for myself each day. It was usually some little thing that was purely for my own enjoyment. One day it would be buying a coffee mocha at the bookstore cafe and browsing through books for an hour. The next night it would be taking a long bath while listening to music, or it was buying myself some flowers, or calling a friend on the East Coast who I hadn't talked to for a while. It could have been any number of things."

Then she explained that she also made it a goal to do something for someone else. "We survivors need to remember there are other people with wounds also. It doesn't take a genius," she said, "to figure out one thing you can do to make the day better for another person. And it doesn't have to consume a lot of time, or any money." Then she went on to explain that she used this reward behavior for herself and those around her to jolt herself loose from feelings of hopelessness and desolation. "Before I realized it," she said, "I'd dramatically changed the tone of my life."

By engaging in small acts to reward ourselves and others, we can replace our own state of despair with one of personal reward and competency.

༄ *My future is not some big conglomeration of punishing tomorrows. It is a series of days in which there are opportunities for me to give and receive small but meaningful pleasures. I will not see myself as the victim of my future but as its architect.*

I don't want to put myself in a position where I might get hurt. I can't take that chance.

And the trouble is, if you don't risk
anything, you risk even *more*.

ERICA JONG

There is a necessary wisdom that allows us, as survivors, to protect ourselves. We don't want to feel any more vulnerable than we already are. We don't want to commit ourselves to doing anything that might require too much strength, endurance, or time, because we're not sure of how we're going to feel. This self-protection serves an important purpose. It allows us to gather enough strength to get on our feet again.

But there comes a time when we rejoin the world. We return to work, reenter the circle of our friends, step out into our neighborhood, or take part in community affairs. During this time we may be conscious of taking risks—risks in new activities, risks in starting new relationships, risks in committing ourselves to something.

But risk is inherent in life, in daily living. Risk is part of anything that is alive. If we don't take chances, if we don't prod ourselves into action when we are reluctant to do something, we're still at risk: We're taking the chance that our lives will be limited, meaningless, and drab. So we must venture out in order to experience our full potential. There is no alternative.

   I know at some point I need to get beyond the safety of inertia, indifference, or denial. I need to engage, to connect, to be part of the world. Even though I may feel, at first, as if I am thrusting myself into unpredictable territory, I will realize that by not doing so I am putting at stake the wholeness of my life.

I know I'll never have that kind of love again.

The supreme happiness of life
is the conviction that we are loved.

VICTOR HUGO

*E*ach person in our life who loves us gives us a love that cannot be duplicated by any other person. If all the people we now love and are loved by expressed and felt exactly the same kind of love toward us, our lives would be less rich.

So although we can no longer receive the unique love that death has taken away from us, we know that we can still experience warmth and affection by accepting and respecting the loving relationships that we do have.

It's hurtful and wrong for us to see ourselves now as unlovable or unloved. Rather, we need to recognize that we are capable of loving in a multitude of ways. Our happiness, in fact, is based on love, and we must not cut ourselves off from the possibility of experiencing new loving relationships in our lives. If we have lost a parent, we may establish a new relationship with a mother or father figure; if we've lost a child, we may begin a relationship with another child who is the same age as the child we lost and who has some of the same interests and needs. If we've lost a sibling, we may reach out to a man or woman who can be a particularly close friend. By doing so we are not trying to substitute one person for the other or to replace one love with another, for that is impossible. We are extending ourselves toward new relationships that will have their own value and reward.

❧ *I have lost a unique and loving relationship that cannot be duplicated. I will recognize that if it could be duplicated, my bond with my loved one would not have been as strong. Now, I will look at the other people from whom I receive love and I will see their love as valuable, as contributing to my happiness, each one's in a special way. And even though I yearn for the love I had, I will not cut myself off from the possibility of having other loving relationships.*

Well, I never really expected my life to turn out like this.

Reality can destroy the dream;
why shouldn't the dream destroy reality?

GEORGE MOORE

*B*efore the death, all of us had our expectations, plans, beliefs, and dreams. Then when the loss occurred, all that had sustained our hopes, given us energy, and propelled us forward became damaged. We may have felt as if our very lives were hopelessly destroyed. But once we went to the bottom of our despair and felt all the horrendous, demanding emotions that accompanied the loss of our loved one, we started to rise again to the surface, to a place where we could allow ourselves a dream.

Now we can reinvent the life we have before us. We can put into it things that are good for ourselves and others. We can make a difference in the world in which we live. We can do it because we believe in the power and the spirit of our own will.

❧ *The reality of my loss stomped around on all that I clung to, all that I had hoped for, all that made my life worthwhile and special. But I can recover from that now. I have been through all the painful aspects of loss. I have submitted myself to the cruel reality of my loved one's death and all that it required of me. Now I will reconstruct my dream, and I will put it in the place where agony once resided. My dream will be as strong as the harshest reality—even stronger, because I gained determination and power as I made my way through the darkest wilderness to get to this place of creation.*

I am finally able to accept the death.

My life appears dispassionate, unhurried, free from pain. . . .
The thought of you and of that . . . love we had holds . . .
no constricting hand about my heart. I know, accept and sleep.
VIOLET TURNER

*A*fter all sorrow, there comes a time of acceptance. We know we don't need to hold so tightly, to cling so violently, to yearn until it pains us. We miss our loved one terribly, but we accept the loss. The death may have come far too soon or in a way that torments us when we think about it. But still, eventually we accept the death into our life. We begin to function somewhat normally—to eat, to sleep, to be able to talk with people. Our life changes as it incorporates the fact of death. Our mind eases as we loosen the bonds that held our loved one to our hearts.

∾ *Tonight if I begin to experience the deep loneliness and hurt that descend more commonly at the end of the day, all those feelings that keep me awake and watchful, I will begin the process of acceptance. I will imagine that the bonds that bind my loved one to me are soft ribbons that I will loosen little by little until I have let go, until I no longer feel their constricting ties about my heart. Doing so does not mean I love less; it means I accept the needs of my body and mind. It means I trust my love enough not to have to hold on until it harms me.*

I am surprised by recurrences of deep grief just when I'm sure I'm better.

Joy and pain can live in the same
house. Neither should deny the other.

TAN NENG

*L*ife seems somewhat whole again. Laughter is possible, even occasional joy. Then one day, without warning, there is a return of the deepest, most wrenching emotions, taking us back to the early days. They cause us to feel confusion about being healed.

But it's not a reason to become discouraged. Such a recurrence is all part of the process. Once the loss of a loved one has marked our life, we are open to episodes of this sort, regardless of how well we may be doing most of the time. There is no use trying to deny this emotion when it wells up. Instead, we need to take some time to acknowledge it. We need to give it our attention. Then we can resume where we left off, pick up where we were interrupted, and allow ourselves to be open to what is happening around us, to what we are feeling and thinking and what we need. Even though the recurrences of deep grief will happen from time to time, they will get further and further apart.

ॐ *When I am taken by surprise by a rush of pain, even in the midst of happiness, I will not try to deny it. Instead, I will acknowledge that it is in my life too, at another level and possibly inactive much of the time, but it is there just the same. I will allow the pain as I allow the joy; I will let them both live in the same house. They each have played and will play an integral part in making my life emotionally honest and whole.*

Finally, one day, I didn't have to force myself anymore.

The heart carries the feet.
HEBREW PROVERB

*D*uring the worst of grief it can seem as if every civilized act, every simple function, even every move we make is forced. Great effort is required to get out of bed, to get from home to work, or sometimes even to get from one side of the room to another. But then, eventually, as we work through our grief, the load that weighed so heavily on us lessens. Tomorrow seems less like an ordeal and more like an opportunity. The dark side of our spirit subsides.

It happens gradually, but it does happen. One day we find that less effort is required for the things that once took an enormous amount of exertion. One day we realize that we again are capable of feeling delight, inspiration, and anticipation.

☙ *I will trust that my burden will continue to dwindle as the days pass and the heaviness I feel lightens. I will have complete faith that there will come a time when I do not need to push myself, with tremendous effort, from one place to another or from one task to another. I will feel then that I have achieved a new strength and that I have a mended heart that can propel me through the demands of tomorrow—a heart that can be trusted to "carry my feet."*

*I have found myself feeling guilty because I was enjoying
something or because I was laughing.*

Laughter can be more satisfying than honor; more
precious than money; more heart cleansing than prayer.
HARRIET ROCHLIN

We may have trouble giving ourselves permission to exhibit enjoyment or to take part in something pleasurable—especially if we are in public. But doing so is an important step toward the resolution of our loss. Taking some pleasure in life does not mean we are being disloyal to our loved one who died. It doesn't mean we no longer care. It doesn't mean we are insensitive. It means that it is time for us to allow our emotions to range toward the positive end of the continuum. Our emotional reactions and conditions do not have to be confined to those connected with our grief. It isn't wrong to rejoin the world of pleasure, to enjoy ourselves, to laugh.

 I won't repress the expression of pleasure. I won't be afraid to join in laughter. I will instead be thankful that I can still experience feelings of joy and that I am able to release them in the company of those I care about. My loved one would not want me to remain mired in only the deepest and darkest of emotions. This transition represents life reaching toward new life—not life continually reaching backward toward death.

Now I am continually reminding myself that I need to make my life mean more.

Look at every path closely and deliberately.
Then ask yourself, Does this path have a heart?
If it does, the path is good; if it doesn't, it is of no use.

CARLOS CASTANEDA

A woman who counsels survivors said, "There are two kinds of people in the world: those who have been through deep grief and those who haven't. When I walk into a room of strangers, I can tell those who have lived through deep grief, for they are the most compassionate, the most human." It's also true that those who are the most human, the most in touch with their inner selves—with the essence of their lives and the meaningful parts of the lives of those closest to them— are those who follow the path that has a heart.

We've learned time and time again that death brings life more clearly into focus and allows us to identify its most valuable assets. These are the assets that do not translate into material gain. As we make important decisions about the way we will lead our future lives in the days ahead, we need to remember that we are free to examine any path we would take, to ask ourselves if the path has a heart, to turn away from it if we see there is no real human value to it. We can ask ourselves, for example, will this path lead me away from the mechanical and material toward the humane? Will it allow me to be a valuable person in this society—one who gives, supports, creates, and nurtures?

❧ *The life ahead of me consists of many paths. I will choose those that fit with what I know to be right and true in my heart. I will use what I have learned from this grief experience to enhance the inner quality of my own life and the lives of those around me.*

I'm doing things that seem worthwhile and that give me great pleasure.

Happiness is not a goal, it is a by-product.
ELEANOR ROOSEVELT

A man who survived the loss of his son to AIDS talked of what grief taught him about happiness. "Before I went through the loss of my son, I didn't focus on what was important. In fact, the whole family revolved around me and I didn't realize it. Now, it's the opposite. We're all reaching out and involved with those around us. We're working in the community to help other people, and none of us has ever been happier."

Happiness does not come through self-gratification. As we work toward something we know to be right, to be true, as we stop to listen to and assist someone who needs companionship, we will experience more happiness than any activity that is centered on the self could possibly bring us.

❧ *I understand that my happiness is a by-product of my life. The way in which I live my life, the things I do, the problems I solve, the contributions I make, and the sorrows I ease in others all contribute to my own happiness. By thinking not about my happiness, but about the happiness of others, I will achieve my own.*

I honestly don't believe it [life] ends here.

Nature does not know extinction;
all it knows is transformation.

WERNHER VON BRAUN

Some of us have unshakable beliefs. One of the beliefs most common among survivors is that our loved one does not "end" with death. There is, as Wernher von Braun has asserted, "the continuity of our spiritual existence after death." How this works, why it works, how we know, how we don't know—all this remains unimportant. What is important is the knowledge that what we may see as a finality on earth does not translate into a finality elsewhere.

Many people have discussed their near-death experiences in which they had a loving, welcoming, peaceful entrance into the next realm. They say they saw their loved one who predeceased them. Some of us believe that these reports prove the existence of an afterlife; others of us do not. But most everyone agrees that there is something unexplainable that goes beyond life as we know it here.

❧ *When I think of death, I will also think of life, of the life that continues on after the body is no longer here. I am grateful that my loved one is and always will be, regardless of the death that occurred on earth. Death is not termination, it is transformation.*

I'm finally able to go to the cemetery and feel at peace with myself.

Ah! If you only knew the peace
there is in an accepted sorrow.
JEANNE DE LA MOTTE-GUYON

*I*t is a long, hard road we have had to walk before reaching a place of relative tranquility. But once here, we do experience relief and release from our greatest despair. The death of a loved one is not something we ever "get over," but after working through our grief, giving ourselves time to feel the sorrow, viewing our own lives from their changed perspective, we are able to accept, at last, what has happened to us. This is the gift we have given ourselves by sticking with the grief and working it through, instead of denying it or transforming it into something it isn't.

Those who run away from grief never achieve any inner peace. But because we have confronted our loss, it is now possible for us to lead our lives free—or relatively free, at least—of inner conflict. As one widower remarked, "I can go to her grave now with flowers and peace in my heart, instead of flowers in my hands and thorns in my heart."

❧ *By confronting my loss, I have enabled myself to achieve a sense of peace. If not today, I will be able one day in the future to accept my sorrow. I will work toward that acceptance. Now I will congratulate myself for coming this far, for confronting the whole painful array of grief-related feelings and conditions, and working them through.*

She is always here with me. She is in my life every day, all day.

To live in hearts we leave,
Is not to die.
THOMAS CAMPBELL

The lasting gift that any loved one gives us is their presence in our hearts. The memories and the very spirit of the person live on in us, and in the things we cherish and do, long after the person is no longer physically here. That is something no one can ever take away from us.

We can acknowledge that our loved one will always be with us, that during times when we are severely tested, when we are feeling weak or particularly vulnerable, we can remember that our loved one is with us in ways that are not visible. This presence can be a source of comfort or sustenance, of strength or beauty. It is up to us to dedicate ourselves to integrating that loving spirit into our ongoing lives.

❧ *I will feel sustained knowing that my loved one is with me now and will be present always in my heart. For that presence I will be thankful.*

Index